SPSS

SPSS® 6.1
Base System User's Guide, Part 1
Macintosh® Version

SPSS Inc.

SPSS Inc.
444 N. Michigan Avenue
Chicago, Illinois 60611
Tel: (312) 329-2400
Fax: (312) 329-3668

SPSS Federal Systems (U.S.)
SPSS Latin America
SPSS Benelux BV
SPSS GmbH Software
SPSS UK Ltd.
SPSS France SARL
SPSS Hispanoportuguesa S. L.
SPSS Scandinavia AB
SPSS India Private Ltd.
SPSS Asia Pacific Pte. Ltd.
SPSS Japan Inc.
SPSS Australasia Pty. Ltd.

For more information about SPSS® software products, please write or call

Marketing Department
SPSS Inc.
444 North Michigan Avenue
Chicago, IL 60611
Tel: (312) 329-2400
Fax: (312) 329-3668

SPSS is a registered trademark and the other product names are the trademarks of SPSS Inc. for its proprietary computer software. No material describing such software may be produced or distributed without the written permission of the owners of the trademark and license rights in the software and the copyrights in the published materials.

The SOFTWARE and documentation are provided with RESTRICTED RIGHTS. Use, duplication, or disclosure by the Government is subject to restrictions as set forth in subdivision (c)(1)(ii) of The Rights in Technical Data and Computer Software clause at 52.227-7013. Contractor/manufacturer is SPSS Inc., 444 N. Michigan Avenue, Chicago, IL 60611.

General notice: Other product names mentioned herein are used for identification purposes only and may be trademarks of their respective companies.

Macintosh and AppleScript are registered trademarks of Apple Computer, Inc.

SPSS® 6.1 Base System User's Guide, Part 1, Macintosh® Version
Copyright © 1994 by SPSS Inc.
All rights reserved.
Printed in the United States of America.

1 2 3 4 5 6 7 8 9 0   96 95 94

ISBN 0-13-438862-3

Preface

SPSS is a comprehensive and flexible statistical analysis and data management system. SPSS can take data from almost any type of file and use them to generate tabulated reports, charts, and plots of distributions and trends, descriptive statistics, and complex statistical analyses.

SPSS for the Macintosh provides a user interface that makes statistical analysis accessible for the casual user and convenient for the experienced user. Simple menus and dialog box selections make it possible to perform complex analyses without typing a single line of command syntax. The Data Editor offers a simple and efficient spreadsheet-like facility for entering data and browsing the working data file. High-resolution, presentation-quality charts and plots are included as part of the Base system.

This manual, the *SPSS Base System User's Guide, Part 1, Macintosh Version,* documents the graphical user interface of SPSS for the Macintosh. The *SPSS Base System User's Guide, Part 2* documents in detail the procedures on the Statistics menu and the Graphs menu. Beneath the menus and dialog boxes, SPSS uses a command language, and some features of the system can be accessed only via command syntax. Complete command syntax is documented in the *SPSS Base System Syntax Reference Guide*.

SPSS Options

The SPSS family of products includes add-on enhancements to the SPSS Base system, which are available on several computer platforms. Contact your local SPSS office or sales representative about availability of the following options:

- **SPSS Professional Statistics**™ provides techniques to measure the similarities and differences in data, classify data, identify underlying dimensions, and more. It includes procedures for these analyses: cluster, k-means cluster, discriminant, factor, multidimensional scaling, proximity, and reliability.
- **SPSS Advanced Statistics**™ includes sophisticated techniques such as logistic regression, loglinear analysis, multivariate analysis of variance, constrained nonlinear regression, probit analysis, Cox regression, and Kaplan-Meier and actuarial survival analysis.
- **SPSS Tables**™ creates a variety of presentation-quality tabular reports, including complex stub-and-banner tables and displays of multiple response data.

- **SPSS Trends**™ performs comprehensive forecasting and time series analyses with multiple curve-fitting models, smoothing models, and methods for estimating autoregressive functions.
- **SPSS Categories**™ performs conjoint analysis and optimal scaling procedures, including correspondence analysis.
- **SPSS CHAID**™ simplifies tabular analysis of categorical data, develops predictive models, screens out extraneous predictor variables, and produces easy-to-read tree diagrams that segment a population into subgroups that share similar characteristics.
- **SPSS LISREL**® 7 analyzes linear structural relations and simultaneous equation models.

Compatibility

The SPSS Base system is designed to operate on many computer systems. See the installation instructions that came with your system for specific information on minimum and recommended requirements.

Serial Numbers

Your serial number is your identification number with SPSS Inc. You will need this serial number when you call SPSS Inc. for information regarding support, payment, a defective diskette, or an upgraded system.

The serial number can be found on the diskette labeled Installation that came with your Base system. Before using the system, please copy this number to the registration card.

Registration Card

STOP! Before continuing on, *fill out and send us your registration card*. Until we receive your registration card, you have an unregistered system. Even if you have previously sent a card to us, please fill out and return the card enclosed in your Base system package. Registering your system entitles you to:

- Technical support services

- Favored customer status

- New product announcements

Don't put it off—send your registration card now!

Customer Service

Contact Customer Service at 1-800-521-1337 if you have any questions concerning your shipment or account. Please have your serial number ready for identification when calling.

Training Seminars

SPSS Inc. provides both public and onsite training seminars for SPSS. All seminars feature hands-on workshops. SPSS seminars will be offered in major U.S. and European cities on a regular basis. For more information on these seminars, call the SPSS Inc. Training Department toll-free at 1-800-543-6607.

Technical Support

The services of SPSS Technical Support are available to registered customers of SPSS. Customers may call Technical Support for assistance in using SPSS products or for installation help for one of the supported hardware environments.

To reach Technical Support, call 1-312-329-3410. Be prepared to identify yourself, your organization, and the serial number of your system.

If you are a Value Plus or Customer EXPress customer, use the priority 800 number you received with your materials. For information on subscribing to the Value Plus or Customer EXPress plan, call SPSS Software Sales at 1-800-543-2185.

Additional Publications

Additional copies of SPSS product manuals may be purchased from Prentice Hall, the exclusive distributor of SPSS publications. To order, fill out and mail the Publications order form included with your system, or call toll-free. If you represent a bookstore or have an account with Prentice Hall, call 1-800-223-1360. If you are not an account customer, call 1-800-374-1200. In Canada, call 1-800-567-3800. Outside of North America, contact your local Prentice Hall office.

Lend Us Your Thoughts

Your comments are important. So send us a letter and let us know about your experiences with SPSS products. We especially like to hear about new and interesting applications using the SPSS system. Write to SPSS Inc. Marketing Department, Attn: Micro Software Products Manager, 444 N. Michigan Avenue, Chicago, IL 60611.

Contacting SPSS Inc.

If you would like to be on our mailing list, write to us at one of the addresses below. We will send you a copy of our newsletter and let you know about SPSS Inc. activities in your area.

SPSS Inc.
444 North Michigan Ave.
Chicago, IL 60611
Tel: (312) 329-2400
Fax: (312) 329-3668

SPSS Federal Systems
Courthouse Place
2000 North 14th St.
Suite 320
Arlington, VA 22201
Tel: (703) 527-6777
Fax: (703) 527-6866

SPSS Latin America
444 North Michigan Ave.
Chicago, IL 60611
Tel: (312) 494-3226
Fax: (312) 494-3227

SPSS Benelux BV
P.O. Box 115
4200 AC Gorinchem
The Netherlands
Tel: +31.1830.36711
Fax: +31.1830.35839

SPSS GmbH Software
Rosenheimer Strasse 30
D-81669 Munich
Germany
Tel: +49.89.4890740
Fax: +49.89.4483115

SPSS UK Ltd.
SPSS House
5 London Street
Chertsey
Surrey KT16 8AP
United Kingdom
Tel: +44.1932.566262
Fax: +44.1932.567020

SPSS France SARL
72-74 Avenue Edouard Vaillant
92100 Boulogne
France
Tel: +33.1.4684.0072
Fax: +33.1.4684.0180

SPSS Hispanoportuguesa S.L.
Paseo Pintor Rosales, 26-4
28008 Madrid
Spain
Tel: +34.1.547.3703
Fax: +34.1.548.1346

SPSS Scandinavia AB
Gamla Brogatan 36-38
4th Floor
111 20 Stockholm
Sweden
Tel: +46.8.102610
Fax: +46.8.102550

SPSS India Private Ltd.
Ashok Hotel, Suite 223
50B Chanakyapuri
New Delhi 110 021
India
Tel: +91.11.600121 x1029
Fax: +91.11.688.8851

SPSS Asia Pacific Pte. Ltd.
10 Anson Road, #34-07
International Plaza
Singapore 0207
Singapore
Tel: +65.221.2577
Fax: +65.221.9920

SPSS Japan Inc.
2-2-22 Jingu-mae
Shibuya-ku, Tokyo
150 Japan
Tel: +81.3.5474.0341
Fax: +81.3.5474.2678

SPSS Australasia Pty. Ltd.
121 Walker Street
North Sydney, NSW 2060
Australia
Tel: +61.2.954.5660
Fax: +61.2.954.5616

Contents

7   Modifying Chart Elements: Chart Menu   121

1

Overview of SPSS for the Macintosh

SPSS provides a powerful statistical analysis and data management system in a graphical environment, using descriptive menus and simple dialog boxes to do most of the work for you. Most tasks can be accomplished simply by pointing and clicking the mouse.

In addition to the menu-driven dialog box interface for statistical analysis, SPSS provides:

- **Data Editor.** A versatile spreadsheet-like system for defining, entering, editing, and displaying data.
- **Chart Editor.** A highly visual, object-oriented facility for manipulating and customizing the many charts and graphs produced by SPSS.
- **High-resolution graphics.** High-resolution, full-color pie charts, bar charts, histograms, scatterplots, 3-D graphics, and more are now included as a standard feature in the SPSS Base system.

Getting Started

The SPSS folder, created when you install SPSS, is shown in Figure 1.1.

Figure 1.1   SPSS folder

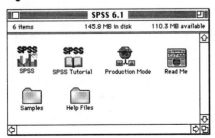

To start an SPSS session, double-click the mouse on the SPSS icon. This opens an output window and the Data Editor window, as shown in Figure 1.2.

Figure 1.2   SPSS output and Data Editor windows

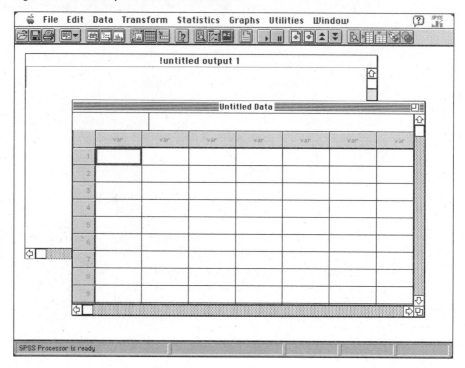

Online Tutorial

The online tutorial introduces you to SPSS concepts and provides instructions for performing tasks in SPSS. To run the tutorial, double-click the SPSS tutorial icon in the SPSS folder.

You can select a topic or use the controls at the bottom of the window to navigate within the tutorial. The main menu and topic menus allow you to go directly to the topic that interests you. You can exit from the tutorial at any time. Further instructions for using the tutorial are provided within the tutorial itself.

SPSS Windows

There are five types of windows in SPSS:

Output window. As you make selections from the menus and dialog boxes, various system information and the text-based results of your work—such as descriptive statistics, crosstabulations, or correlation matrices—appear in an output window. You can edit this output and save it in files for later use. An output window opens automatically when you start a new SPSS session. You can also open additional output windows.

Data Editor window. This window displays the contents of the data file. You can create new data files or modify existing ones with the Data Editor. The Data Editor window opens automatically when you start an SPSS session.

Chart Carousel window. All of the charts and graphs produced in your SPSS session are accessed through the Chart Carousel, which opens automatically the first time you generate a chart during the session. If you produce multiple charts, you can view them in the Chart Carousel before modifying, saving, or discarding them.

Chart window. You can modify and save high-resolution charts and plots in chart windows. You can change the colors, select different type fonts or sizes, switch the horizontal and vertical axes, rotate 3-D scatterplots, and even change the chart type.

Syntax window. You can paste your dialog box choices into a syntax window, where your selections appear in the form of command syntax. You can then edit the command syntax to utilize special features of SPSS not available through dialog boxes. You can save these commands in a file for use in subsequent SPSS sessions. You can open multiple syntax windows.

Designated versus Active Window

If you have more than one open output window, the text-based results of your work are routed to the **designated** output window. If you have more than one open syntax window, command syntax is pasted into the designated syntax window. The designated windows are indicated by an exclamation point (!) in the title bar. You can change the designated windows at any time (see "Toolbar" on p. 5).

The designated window should not be confused with the **active** window, which is the currently selected window. If you have overlapping windows, the active window appears in the foreground. If you open a new syntax or output window, that window automatically becomes the active window, but it does not become the designated window until you instruct SPSS to make it the designated window.

Main Menu

Most of the features in SPSS can be accessed by making selections from the menus. The following menus are available:

File. Use the File menu to open, print, and save data files and results, apply formats or templates from other files, close files, and quit SPSS.

Edit. Use the Edit menu to modify or copy text from the output or syntax windows.

Data. Use the Data menu to make global changes to SPSS data files, such as merging files, transposing variables and cases, or creating subsets of cases for analysis. These changes are only temporary and do not affect the permanent file unless you explicitly save the file with the changes.

Transform. Use the Transform menu to make changes to selected variables in the data file and to compute new variables based on the values of existing ones. These changes do not affect the permanent file unless you explicitly save the changes.

Statistics. Use the Statistics menu to select the various statistical procedures you want to use, such as crosstabulation, analysis of variance, correlation, and linear regression.

Graphs. Use the Graphs menu to create bar charts, pie charts, histograms, scatterplots, and other full-color, high-resolution graphs. Some statistical procedures also generate graphs. All graphs can be customized with the Chart Editor.

Utilities. Use the Utilities menu to change fonts, display information about the contents of SPSS data files, or open an index of SPSS commands.

Window. Use the Window menu to arrange, select, and control the attributes of the various SPSS windows.

Chart Menus

The Chart Carousel and chart windows provide different sets of menus for reviewing and editing charts. These menus replace the main menu bar if the Chart Carousel or chart window is the active window. For more information on these menus, see Chapter 6 through Chapter 8.

Help Menu

 The Balloon Help icon on the menu bar provides the following online Help options:

Show Balloons. Displays pop-up balloons with brief descriptions of SPSS menus and toolbar features. After you turn on Balloon Help, point the mouse cursor at the menu selection or tool that you want to know about. Balloon Help is also available for dialog boxes that don't have a Help button.

SPSS Help. Displays the table of contents for the SPSS online Help system. You can select a topic from the list or search for help on a specific topic or keyword.

Toolbar

The toolbar provides quick, easy access to many powerful features that you may use frequently. Figure 1.3 shows the toolbar.

Figure 1.3   Toolbar

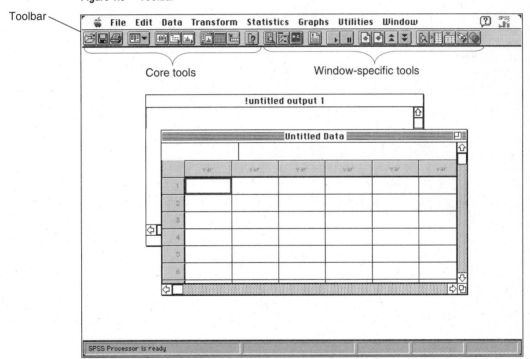

The toolbar contains **core tools** that are available when any type of window is active and **window-specific tools** that change as different types of windows are activated.

Core Tools

The tools described in this section are available when any type of window is active. The core tools are shown in Figure 1.4.

Figure 1.4   Core tools

 File Open. Displays a dialog box for selecting and opening files.

 File Save. Saves the file in the active window. For new documents, displays a dialog box for saving files.

 File Print. Displays the Print dialog box for the type of document that is in the active window.

 Dialog Recall. Displays a list of recently opened dialog boxes, as shown in Figure 1.5. To display one of the dialog boxes on the list, click on its name.

Figure 1.5   List of recently opened dialog boxes

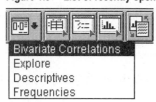

 Cycle through Output. Activates the next output window in the stack of windows.

 Cycle through Syntax. Activates the next syntax window in the stack of windows.

 Cycle through Charts. Activates the next chart in the stack of windows, including the Chart Carousel. It does not cycle through the charts within the Chart Carousel.

 Go to Chart. When an output window is active, this tool activates the chart that corresponds to the next high-resolution chart line in the output window.

 Go to Output. When a chart window is active, this tool highlights the line in the output window that corresponds to the displayed chart.

Go to Data. Activates the Data Editor. When a point is selected on a chart that is still linked to the data, clicking on this tool activates the Data Editor and displays the highlighted case associated with the selected point.

 Go to Case. Displays the Go to Case dialog box. You can use it to scroll to a case in the Data Editor.

 Variable Information. Displays the Variables dialog box. In the Variables dialog box, you can see the variable label, variable type, missing values, and value labels for any selected variable.

Window-Specific Tools

The tools described in this section are available when a data, output, or syntax window is active. The toolbar for these types of windows is shown in Figure 1.6.

Figure 1.6   Toolbar for data, output, or syntax window

 Search for Text. Displays the Search for Text dialog box, which you can use to search for text strings in an output or syntax window.

 Syntax Help. If an SPSS command is selected, this tool displays the associated syntax chart. If no command is selected, an index of SPSS commands is displayed.

 Glossary. Displays a definition of a selected term in an output window. If no text is selected, or if no glossary entry matches the selected term, a Help search index of glossary entries is displayed. Each glossary entry describes a term found in SPSS output. The glossary is displayed in a Help window.

 Designate Window. If a syntax window is active, this tool designates the window as the one to receive syntax when you click on **Paste** in dialog boxes. If an output window is active, this tool designates the window as the one to receive output when you execute an SPSS procedure. In either case, it puts an exclamation point at the beginning of the window title.

 Run Syntax. In a syntax window, this tool runs commands that are selected or, if there is no selection, the command in which the insertion point is positioned.

 Pause/Scroll. In an output window, this tool pauses the scrolling of output in the window. Click on it again to restart the scrolling of output.

Page Up. In an output window, this tool scrolls up one page. Page headers must be turned on (or page markers must be inserted manually) for this feature to work. See Chapter 11 for information about output preferences and page headers.

 Page Down. In an output window, this tool scrolls down one page.

 Block Up. In an output window, clicking on this tool scrolls to the previous block of output. Each SPSS procedure that you run creates an output block. The start of each output block is marked with a small hollow diamond.

 Block Down. In an output window, clicking on this tool scrolls to the next block of output.

 Search for Data. Opens the Search for Data dialog box, which you can use to search for a data value in the selected variable in the Data Editor.

 Insert Case. In the Data Editor, clicking on this tool inserts a case above the case containing the active cell.

 Insert Variable. In the Data Editor, clicking on this tool inserts a variable to the left of the variable containing the active cell.

 Value Labels. Toggles between actual values and value labels in the Data Editor.

 Use Sets. Opens the Use Sets dialog box. You can select the sets of variables to be displayed in the dialog boxes.

Chart Tools

The chart tools, shown in Figure 1.7, are available when a chart window is active.

Figure 1.7   Chart tools

 Point Selection Mode. Toggles between point selection mode and chart edit mode.

 Bar Style. Opens the Bar Styles palette, which allows you to add a drop shadow or a 3-D effect to a bar chart.

Bar Label Style. Opens the Bar Label Styles palette, which allows you to label each bar on a bar chart with its numerical value.

 Interpolation. Opens the Line Interpolation palette, which allows you to connect the data points on a line chart or scatterplot.

 3-D Rotation. Opens the 3-D Rotation dialog box, which allows you to rotate a 3-D scatterplot.

 Swap Axes. Swaps the axes on a 2-D chart, which changes the orientation between vertical and horizontal.

 Explode Slice. Separates one or more slices from a pie chart for emphasis.

 Break Lines at Missing. Allows you to control whether line charts have a break where missing values should be.

 Options. Opens the Options dialog box for the type of chart that is in the active window.

 Spin Mode. When a 3-D scatterplot is in the active window, this tool changes the chart to spin mode, where the chart is displayed with only the tripod and points.

Status Bar

The status bar indicates the current status of the SPSS Processor. If the Processor is running a command, it displays the command name and a case counter indicating the current case number being processed. When you first begin an SPSS session, the status bar displays the message Starting SPSS Processor. When SPSS is ready, the message changes to SPSS Processor is ready. The status bar also provides the following information:

- **Command status.** For each procedure or command you run, a case counter indicates the number of cases processed so far. For statistical procedures that require iterative processing, the number of iterations is displayed.
- **Filter status.** If you have selected a random sample or a subset of cases for analysis, the message Filter on indicates that some type of case filtering is currently in effect and not all cases in the data file are included in the analysis.
- **Weight status.** The message Weight on indicates that a weight variable is being used to weight cases for analysis.
- **Split File status.** The message Split File on indicates that the data file has been split into separate groups for analysis, based on the values of one or more grouping variables.

Data Editor

The Data Editor provides a convenient spreadsheet-like facility for entering, editing, and displaying the contents of your data file.

The Data Editor opens automatically when you start an SPSS session. If there isn't an open data file, you can use the Data Editor to create one. If there is an open data file, you can use the Data Editor to change data values and add or delete cases and variables.

The Data Editor has many similarities to a spreadsheet program, but there are several important distinctions:

- Rows represent cases.
- Columns represent variables.
- There are no "empty" cells within the boundaries of the data file. For numeric variables, blank cells are converted to the system-missing value (represented by a period). For string variables, a blank is considered a valid value.

Figure 1.8 shows a data file displayed in the Data Editor.

Figure 1.8   Data Editor window

	id	salbeg	sex	time	age	salnow	edlevel	work	jobcat	minority
1	628	8400	0	81	28.50	16080	16	.25	4	0
2	630	24000	0	73	40.33	41400	16	12.50	5	0
3	632	10200	0	83	31.08	21960	15	4.08	5	0
4	633	8700	0	93	31.17	19200	16	1.83	4	0
5	635	17400	0	83	41.92	28350	19	13.00	5	0
6	637	12996	0	80	29.50	27250	18	2.42	4	0
7	641	6900	0	79	28.00	16080	15	3.17	1	0
8	649	5400	0	67	28.75	14100	15	.50	1	0
9	650	5040	0	96	27.42	12420	15	1.17	1	0
10	652	6300	0	77	52.92	12300	12	26.42	3	0
11	653	6300	0	84	33.50	15720	15	6.00	1	0
12	656	6000	0	88	54.33	8880	12	27.00	1	0
13	657	10500	0	93	32.33	22000	17	2.67	4	0
14	658	10800	0	98	41.17	22800	15	12.00	5	0
15	659	13200	0	64	31.92	19020	19	2.25	5	0

Bank Employee Data — 17:id — 669

For a complete discussion of the Data Editor, see Chapter 3.

Statistical Analysis with the Dialog Box Interface

There are three basic steps in performing statistical analysis with SPSS:

- Get your data into SPSS. This can be a data file you create with the Data Editor, a previously defined SPSS data file, a spreadsheet file, a database file, or a text file. The contents of the data file are displayed in the Data Editor.
- Choose a statistical procedure from the menus.
- Choose the variables to include in the analysis and any additional parameters from the dialog boxes.

Choosing a Statistical Procedure

Use the Statistics menu to select statistical procedures. The Statistics menu, shown in Figure 1.9, contains a list of general statistical categories. Each of these is followed by an arrow (▶), which indicates that there is another menu level. The individual statistical procedures are listed at this submenu level.

Figure 1.9   Statistics menu

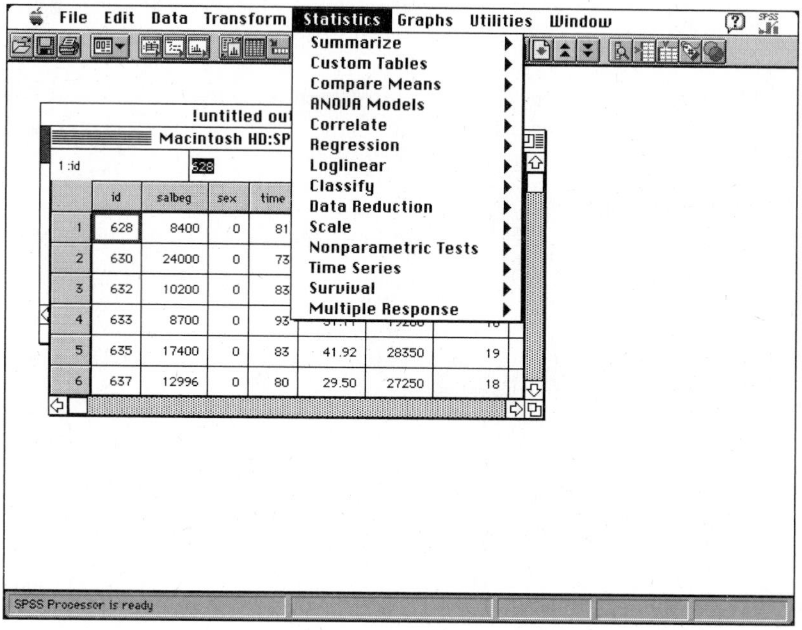

Using Dialog Boxes

When you choose a statistical or chart procedure from the menus, a dialog box appears on the screen. Figure 1.10 shows the Frequencies dialog box.

Figure 1.10   Frequencies main dialog box

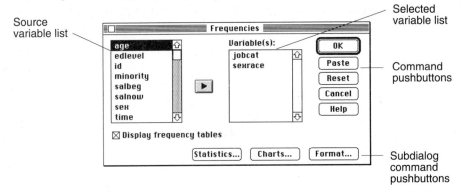

The main dialog box for each statistical procedure has three basic components:

Source variable list. A list of variables in the data file.

Selected variable list(s). One or more lists indicating the variables you have chosen for the analysis, such as dependent and independent variable lists. This is sometimes referred to as the target variable list.

Command pushbuttons. Action buttons that tell SPSS to do something, such as run the procedure, get help, or go to a subdialog box for additional specifications.

Source Variable List

The source variable list contains any variables in the data file that can be used by that procedure. There are three basic types of variables:

- **Numeric variables.** This includes any variables that use a numeric coding scheme, even if the underlying "real" values are not numeric. Date and time format variables are also considered numeric because they are stored internally as a number of seconds.

- **Short string variables.** Alphanumeric string values up to eight characters long. These are identified with a "less than" symbol (<).

- **Long string variables.** Alphanumeric string values more than eight characters long. These are identified with a "greater than" symbol (>).

Standard Controls

Most main dialog boxes have five standard pushbutton controls:

OK. Runs the procedure. After you select your variables and choose any additional specifications, click on OK to run the procedure. This also closes the dialog box.

Paste. Generates command syntax from the dialog box selections and pastes the syntax into a syntax window. You can then customize the commands with additional SPSS features not available from dialog boxes.

Reset. Deselects any variables in the selected variable list(s) and resets all specifications in the dialog box and any subdialog boxes to the default state.

Cancel. Cancels any changes in the dialog box settings since the last time it was opened and closes the dialog box. Within an SPSS session, dialog box settings are persistent. A dialog box retains your last set of specifications until you override them. (See "Persistence of Settings" on p. 15.)

Help. Context-sensitive help. This takes you to a Help window that contains information about the current dialog box.

 Note: Some common Macintosh dialog boxes (such as dialog boxes for opening, printing, and saving files) don't have a Help button. For dialog boxes that don't have a Help button, you can use Balloon Help on the menu bar.

Selecting Variables

To select a single variable, you simply highlight it on the source variable list and click on the ▶ button next to the selected variable list box. If there is only one selected variable list (as in the Frequencies dialog box), you can double-click on individual variables to move them from the source list to the selected list.

You can also select multiple variables:

- To highlight multiple variables that are grouped together on the variable list, as shown in Figure 1.11, click on the first one and then shift-click on the last one in the group.

- To highlight multiple variables that are not grouped together on the variable list, as shown in Figure 1.12, use the command-click method. Click on the first variable, then command-click on the next variable, and so on.

Figure 1.11   Selecting a group of variables with shift-click

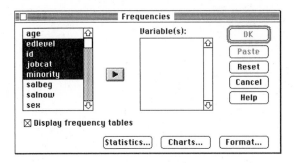

Figure 1.12   Selecting noncontiguous multiple variables with command-click

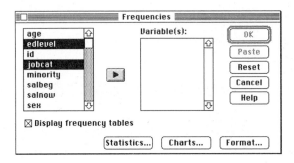

Deselecting Variables

You can also deselect variables, removing them from the selected list and putting them back onto the source list. Deselecting variables works just like selecting them. When you highlight variables on the selected variable list, the ▶ pushbutton changes direction, pointing back to the source variable list.

Subdialog Boxes

Since most SPSS procedures provide a great deal of flexibility, not all of the possible choices can be contained in a single dialog box. The main dialog box usually contains the minimum information required to run a procedure. Additional specifications are made in subdialog boxes.

In the main dialog box, pushbuttons with an ellipsis after the name indicate a subdialog box. For example, the Frequencies main dialog box has three associated subdialog boxes: Statistics, Charts, and Format.

Running a Procedure

In many instances, all you need to do to run a statistical procedure is select your variables and click on OK. The results then appear in the output window, as shown in Figure 1.13.

Figure 1.13 Results displayed in the output window

```
┌─────────────────────────!untitled output─────────────────────┐
│ JOBCAT     Employment category                                │
│                                                               │
│                                                               │
│                                             Valid    Cum       │
│ Value Label           Value  Frequency  Percent  Percent  Percent │
│                                                               │
│ Clerical                1       227     47.9     47.9    47.9  │
│ Office trainee          2       136     28.7     28.7    76.6  │
│ Security officer        3        27      5.7      5.7    82.3  │
│ College trainee         4        41      8.6      8.6    90.9  │
│ Exempt employee         5        32      6.8      6.8    97.7  │
│ MBA trainee             6         5      1.1      1.1    98.7  │
│ Technical               7         6      1.3      1.3   100.0  │
│                                -------  -------  -------        │
│                       Total     474    100.0    100.0          │
│                                                               │
│ Valid cases     474    Missing cases      0                   │
│                                                               │
└───────────────────────────────────────────────────────────────┘
```

Persistence of Settings

Once you click on OK or Paste in a dialog box, the current dialog and subdialog selections are saved. The next time you open that dialog box, those are the settings in effect.

At the subdialog box level, any changes you make are temporarily saved when you click on Continue. If, however, you then click on Cancel in the main dialog box, the subdialog selections revert to their former settings. As with the main dialog box, the subdialog box selections are persistent only after you click on OK or Paste.

The Reset button always returns all dialog and subdialog settings to the default state. You cannot undo this action. (The Cancel button has no effect on Reset.)

Dialog box settings are not persistent for different data files in the same SPSS session. If you make dialog box selections using one data file and then open a different data file, all dialog boxes are reset to the default state with no selected variables.

Order of Operations

For most procedures, you can make your dialog box selections in virtually any order. You can change the selected variable list (or any other setting) in the main dialog box after you make selections in the subdialog boxes, and you can go to subdialog boxes in any sequence. You can even make subdialog box selections before you choose any variables for analysis.

Creating and Editing Charts

If you run a procedure that produces charts or graphs, SPSS displays the results in the Chart Carousel. You can then select the chart and edit it in a chart window. For example, Figure 1.14 shows a bar chart created by the Frequencies procedure.

Figure 1.14   Chart Carousel

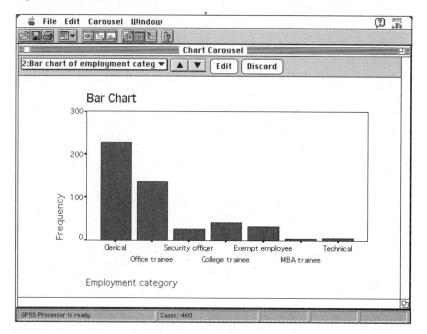

To modify a chart, click on Edit on the Chart Carousel toolbar. The chart is displayed in a chart window.

The SPSS menu bar and toolbar change when a chart window is active, providing a set of features for editing charts. Figure 1.15 shows a modified version of the bar chart.

Figure 1.15   Modified chart

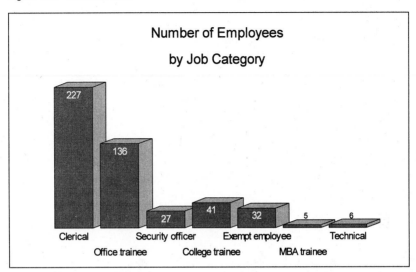

For more information on creating and editing charts and plots, see Chapter 5 through Chapter 8.

Pasting and Editing Command Syntax

The dialog box interface is designed to handle most of the capabilities of SPSS. Beneath the dialog boxes, there is a command language that you can use to access additional features and customize your analysis.

The SPSS command language consists of descriptive and usually self-explanatory commands. For example, the command to obtain frequency tables is FREQUENCIES.

After you make your dialog box selections, you can paste the underlying command syntax into a syntax window. You can then edit the resulting text like any text file and run the modified commands.

- Use the Paste pushbutton in the main dialog box to paste the command syntax into a syntax window.

- Use the Run Syntax tool on the toolbar when a syntax window is active to run the modified commands.

If you don't have an open syntax window, one opens automatically when you paste your syntax. Figure 1.16 shows the FREQUENCIES command syntax pasted into a syntax window.

Figure 1.16   Command syntax pasted into a syntax window

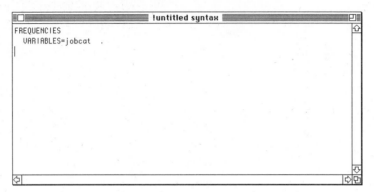

For a complete discussion of editing text files with SPSS and running commands from a syntax window, see Chapter 4.

Saving Results

Data files. You can save data files in SPSS, spreadsheet, database, or text format (see Chapter 2).

Output window results. The output window contains the text-based results of your SPSS session. You can edit this output and save it for later use (see Chapter 4).

Syntax window commands. You can edit and save the command syntax that you paste into a syntax window. You can then recall and rerun these commands in other SPSS sessions or process the commands in production mode (see Appendix A).

Charts and plots. You can save charts and plots from the Chart Carousel or from chart windows and then recall and edit them in other sessions (see Chapter 5).

Ending an SPSS Session

To end an SPSS session:

1. From the menus choose:

    File
     Quit

2. For each open window, SPSS asks if you want to save the contents before it ends the session. To end the session without saving any changes, click on No for each window. If you click on Yes, SPSS opens the appropriate dialog box for saving each type of file (data, output, syntax, chart).

Using SPSS on a Powerbook

If you are using SPSS on a Powerbook with a 640×400 display, some dialog boxes may not fit on the screen with both the SPSS status bar and toolbar displayed. If you have a problem with dialog boxes that don't fit on the screen, you can turn off the display of the status bar and/or the toolbar from the Window menu. With both the status bar and toolbar turned off, all SPSS dialog boxes should fit on a 640×400 display screen.

Decimal Indicator and Numbers Control Panel Settings

The decimal indicator used in the Data Editor and in results displayed in output windows is determined by the Numbers control panel settings. If you specify anything other than a period as the decimal indicator, SPSS uses a comma as the decimal indicator.

The decimal indicator in the Numbers control panel also affects the display of the system-missing value in the Data Editor and in output windows. If a period is the decimal indicator, a period is also used to represent the system-missing value. If anything other than a period is the decimal indicator, a comma is used to represent the system-missing value.

Regardless of the Numbers control panel settings, a period must be used as the decimal indicator in command syntax and in transformation expressions.

2 Data Files

Data files come in a wide variety of formats, and SPSS is designed to handle many of them, including:

- Spreadsheet files created with Lotus 1-2-3, Excel, and Multiplan.
- Database files created with dBASE and various SQL formats.
- Tab-delimited and other types of ASCII text files.
- SPSS data files created on other operating systems.

Creating a New Data File

If your data are not already in computer files, you can use the Data Editor to enter the data and create an SPSS data file. The Data Editor is a simple, efficient spreadsheet-like facility that opens automatically when you start an SPSS session. For information on the Data Editor, see Chapter 3.

Opening a Data File

To open an SPSS, spreadsheet, dBASE, or tab-delimited data file, from the menus choose:

File
 Open...

This opens a standard dialog box for selecting files. Select the data file you want to open.

File Types

To display only data files of a specific type, select a file type from the pop-up menu.

Show. Select one of the following alternatives from the pop-up menu:

➡ **SPSS Data.** Data files created and/or saved in SPSS for the Macintosh, SPSS for Windows, or SPSS for UNIX, and data files saved in SPSS portable format.

SPSS Release 4 files. Files created with SPSS Release 4.0 for the Macintosh.

Excel spreadsheets. Microsoft Excel (versions 2.2 to 4.0) spreadsheet files.

SPSS does not read Excel 5.0 files directly. To read an Excel 5.0 worksheet into SPSS, first save it as an Excel 4.0 worksheet.

Lotus spreadsheets. Lotus 1-2-3 spreadsheet files, releases 1A, 2.0, and 3.0.

dBASE files. dBASE II-, III-, and IV-format files.

TEXT Files. Displays a list of all TEXT-format files, including SYLK and tab-delimited data files. Tab-delimited files can be opened as data, output, or syntax.

Note: For other types of text data files, use Read ASCII data (see "Reading ASCII Text Data Files" on p. 26).

Options

For Lotus, Excel, SYLK, and tab-delimited files, the following option is available:

❏ **Read variable names.** The values in the first row of the file (or cell range) are used as variable names. If variable names exceed eight characters, they are truncated. If they are not unique, SPSS modifies them. (See "Define Fixed Variables" on p. 27 for rules regarding variable names.)

For Lotus, Excel, and SYLK files, the following option is also available:

Range. User-specified range of cells to read.

- For Lotus files, specify the beginning column letter and row number, two periods, and the ending column letter and row number (for example, A1..K14).
- For Excel files, specify the beginning column letter and row number, a colon, and the ending column letter and row number (for example, A1:K14).
- For SYLK files and Excel files saved in R1C1 display format, specify the beginning and ending cells of the range separated by a colon (for example, R1C1:R14C11).

If you have defined a name for a range of cells in the spreadsheet file, you can enter the name in the Range text box.

How SPSS Reads Spreadsheet Data

An SPSS data file is rectangular. The boundaries (or dimensions) of the data file are determined by the number of cases (rows) and variables (columns). There are no "empty" cells within the boundaries of the data file. All cells have a value, even if that value is "blank." The following general rules apply to reading spreadsheet data:

- Rows are considered cases, and columns are considered variables.
- The number of variables is determined by the last column with any nonblank cells or the total number of nonblank cells in the row containing variable names. If you read

variable names, any columns with a blank cell for the variable name are not included in the data file.

- The number of cases is determined by the last row with any nonblank cells within the column boundaries defined by the number of variables.

- The data type and width for each variable are determined by the column width and data type of the first data cell in the column. Values of other types are converted to the system-missing value. If the first data cell in the column is blank, the global default data type for the spreadsheet (usually numeric) is used.

- For numeric variables, blank cells are converted to the system-missing value, indicated by a period.

- For string variables, a blank is a valid string value, and blank cells are treated as valid string values.

- If you don't read variable names from the spreadsheet, SPSS uses the column letters (A, B, C,...) for variable names for Excel and Lotus files. For SYLK files and Excel files saved in R1C1 display format, SPSS uses the column number preceded by the letter C for variable names (*C1*, *C2*, *C3*,...).

Figure 2.1 and Figure 2.2 show how SPSS reads spreadsheet data with and without variable names.

Figure 2.1   Reading spreadsheet data with variable names

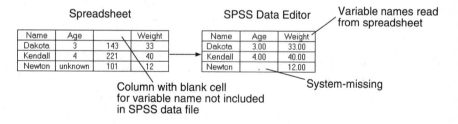

Figure 2.2   Reading an Excel spreadsheet file without variable names

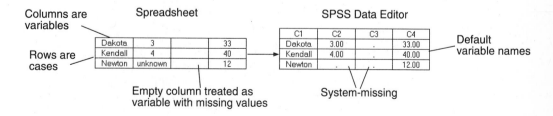

How SPSS Reads dBASE Files

Database files are logically very similar to SPSS data files. The following general rules apply to dBASE files:

- Field names are automatically translated to SPSS variable names.
- Field names should comply with SPSS variable-naming conventions (see "Define Fixed Variables" on p. 27). Field names longer than eight characters are truncated. If the first eight characters of the field name don't produce a unique name, the field is dropped.
- Colons used in dBASE field names are translated to underscores.
- Records marked for deletion but not actually purged are included. SPSS creates a new string variable, *D_R*, which contains an asterisk for cases marked for deletion.

How SPSS Reads Tab-Delimited Files

The following general rules apply to reading tab-delimited files:

- Values can be either numeric or string. Any value that contains non-numeric characters is considered a string value. (Formats such as Dollar and Date are not recognized and are read as string values.)
- The data type and width for each variable are determined by the type and width of the first data value in the column. Values of other types are converted to the system-missing value.
- For numeric variables, the assigned width is eight digits or the number of digits in the first data value, whichever is greater. Values that exceed the defined width are rounded for display. The entire value is stored internally.
- For string variables, values that exceed the defined width are truncated.
- If you don't read variable names from the file, SPSS assigns the default names *var1, var2, var3*, etc.

Data Files Created in SPSS for Windows (and other Windows applications)

Numerous Macintosh utilities exist for reading DOS-format disks, and SPSS for the Macintosh can read data files created in SPSS for Windows (and Windows versions of Excel, Lotus 1-2-3, and dBASE). Here are a few tips that you may find helpful:

- If you use Apple File Exchange, or a similar utility, to read DOS-format disks, make sure that DOS carriage return-line feeds (CR/LF) are converted to simple carriage returns (CR) when SPSS portable or SYLK-format files are copied to the Macintosh. This is default text translation for Apple File Exchange (see Figure 2.3).

- If you use PC Exchange, or a similar utility, to read DOS-format disks, assign a file type of ~SYS to SPSS for Windows data files with a DOS extension of .SAV (see Figure 2.4).

- If your data files created in SPSS for Windows don't appear in the list of readable files in SPSS for the Macintosh, select All Files from the pop-up list of files to show.

Figure 2.3   Reading DOS-format files with Apple File Exchange

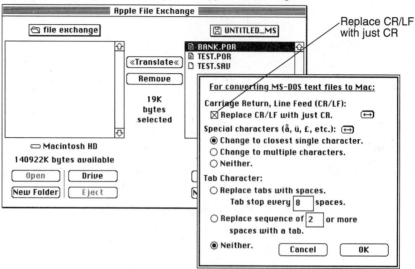

Figure 2.4   Reading DOS-format files with PC Exchange

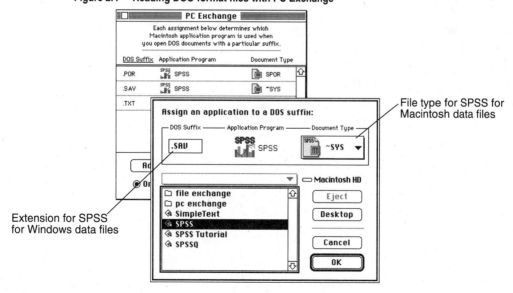

Reading SQL Databases with ODBC

In addition to dBASE database files, with Microsoft ODBC (Open Database Connectivity), SPSS can read can read any database that has an installed ODBC driver. To read a database using ODBC, from the menus choose:

File
  Connect to ODBC Database...

This opens the SQL Data Source dialog box.

Select Data Source. Select the data source from the list of installed data sources. If the data source you want is not on the list, you can use the ODBC Administrator to add data sources. See your Microsoft ODBC documentation for more information.

Depending on the ODBC driver and the requirements of the database, you may have to enter a login ID and/or password before you can access the database.

Variable Names and Labels

The complete database column name is used as the variable label. SPSS assigns variable names to each column from the database in one of two ways:

- If the name of the database column (or the first eight characters) forms a valid, unique SPSS variable name, it is used as the variable name.

- If the name of the database column does not form a valid, unique SPSS variable name, SPSS creates a name by using the first few characters from the column name and adding a numeric suffix, based on the column's position number in the SQL SELECT statement (Fields to Retrieve in the Select Table and Fields dialog box). If the first few characters of the column name are not valid characters for SPSS variable names, the prefix *col* is used with a numeric suffix.

Reading ASCII Text Data Files

If your raw data are in plain text files (standard ASCII format), you can read the data in SPSS and assign variable names and data formats. To read a text file, from the menus choose:

File
  Read ASCII Data...

This opens a standard dialog box for selecting files. Select the ASCII data file you want to read, and then select the file format.

File Format. You can choose one of the following alternatives:

○ **Fixed.** Each variable is recorded in the same column location on the same record (line) for each case in the data file. This is the default.

○ **Freefield.** The variables are recorded in the same order for each case but not necessarily in the same locations. Spaces are interpreted as delimiters between values. More than one case can be recorded on a single line. After reading the value for the last defined variable for a case, SPSS reads the next value encountered as the first variable for the next case.

Define Fixed Variables

To define fixed-format data, select Fixed for the File Format in the Read ASCII Data File dialog box and click on Define. This opens the Define Fixed Variables dialog box, as shown in Figure 2.5.

Figure 2.5   Define Fixed Variables dialog box

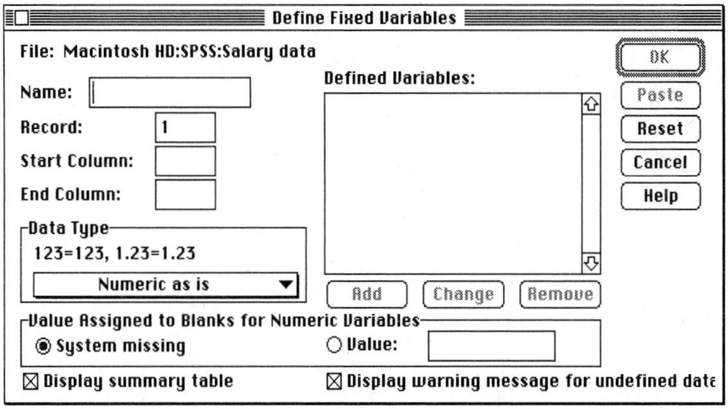

For each variable, you must specify the following:

Name. A variable name must be no more than eight characters long. For detailed rules on variable names, use the online Help system.

The following reserved keywords cannot be used.

ALL	NE	EQ	TO	LE
LT	BY	OR	GT	
AND	NOT	GE	WITH	

Record. A case can have data on more than one line. The **record number** indicates the line within the case where the variable is located.

Start Column/End Column. These two column specifications indicate the location of the variable within the record. The value for a variable can appear anywhere within the range of columns. With the exception of string variables, leading blank spaces in the column range are ignored.

Data Type. As you select each data type, one or more examples of the selected data type are shown above the list in the Data Type box. You can choose one of the following alternatives:

→ **Numeric as is.** Valid values include numbers, a leading plus or minus sign, and a decimal indicator.

Numeric 1 decimal (1). If there is not an explicitly coded decimal indicator, one **implied decimal position** is assigned. For example, 123 is read as 12.3. A value with more than one explicitly coded decimal position (for example, 1.23) is read correctly but is rounded to one decimal position in output unless you change the variable definition (see Chapter 3).

Numeric 2 decimals (2). If there is not an explicitly coded decimal indicator, two implied decimal positions are assigned. For example, 123 is read as 1.23. A value with more than two explicitly coded decimal positions (for example, 1.234) is read correctly but is rounded to two decimal positions in output unless you change the variable definition (see Chapter 3).

Dollar (DOLLAR). Valid values are numbers with an optional leading dollar sign and optional commas as thousands separators. If you don't enter the dollar sign or commas, they are automatically inserted in output. Decimal positions are read but do not appear in output unless you change the variable definition (see Chapter 3). For example, $10.95 would be displayed as $11.

String (A). Valid values include virtually any keyboard characters and imbedded blanks. Leading blanks are treated as part of the value. Internally, string values are right-padded to the total width of the field defined by the Start and End columns. If the defined width is eight or fewer characters, it is a **short string variable**. If the defined width is more than eight characters, it is a **long string variable**. Short string variables can be used in many SPSS procedures; long string variables can be used in fewer procedures.

Date (DATE). Dates of the general format dd-mmm-yyyy. The following conventions apply:

- Dashes, periods, commas, slashes, or blanks can be used as delimiters. For example, 28-10-90, 28/10/1990, 28.OCT.90, and October 28, 1990 are all acceptable.
- Months may be represented in digits, Roman numerals, three-letter abbreviations, or fully spelled out. For example, 10, X, OCT, and October are all acceptable.
- Two-digit years are assumed to have the prefix 19.

Date format variables are displayed with dashes as delimiters and three-letter abbreviations for the month values. Internally, dates are stored as the number of seconds from October 14, 1582.

European Date (EDATE). Dates of the general format dd.mm.yyyy. The conventions for Date format also apply to European Date format. Edate format variables are displayed with slashes as delimiters and numbers for the month values.

American Date (ADATE). Dates of the general format mm/dd/yyyy. The conventions for Date format also apply to American Date. Adate format variables are displayed with slashes as delimiters and numbers for the month values.

Julian Date (JDATE). Dates of the general format yyyyddd. The following rules apply:

- If the input value contains only five digits, a two-digit year is assumed, and 1900 is added.
- Year values can be two or four digits. Two-digit year values less than 10 must contain a leading zero.
- All day values must be three digits. Leading zeros are required for day values less than 100.

Quarter and Year (QYR). Dates of the general format qQyyyy. The quarter is expressed as 1, 2, 3, or 4, and the year is represented by two or four digits. If two digits are used, 1900 is added. The quarter and the year are separated by the letter Q. Blanks may be used as additional delimiters. For example, 4Q90, 4Q1990, 4 Q 90, and 4 Q 1990 are all acceptable.

Month and Year (MOYR). Dates of the general format mm/yyyy. The Date format conventions for month and year apply.

Week and Year (WKYR). Dates of the general form wkWKyyyy. A week is expressed as a number from 1 to 53. Week 1 begins on January 1, week 2 on January 8, and so forth. The year is a two- or four-digit number. If it is a two-digit number, 1900 is added. The week and year are separated by the string WK. Blanks can be used as additional delimiters. For example, 43WK90, 43WK1990, and 43 WK 1990 are all acceptable.

Date and Time (DATETIME). Values containing a date and a time. The following conventions apply:

- The date must be written as an international date (dd-mmm-yyyy) followed by a blank and then a time value in the form hh:mm:ss.ss.
- The time conforms to a 24-hour clock. Thus, the maximum hour value is 23; the maximum minute value is 59; and the seconds value must be less than 60.
- Fractional seconds must have the decimal indicator explicitly coded in the data value.

For example, the input values 25/1/90 1 2, 25-JAN-1990 1:02, and 25 January 1990 01:02:00 are all acceptable variations for the same value.

Time (TIME). Time of day or time interval values of the general form hh:mm:ss.ss. The following conventions apply:

- Colons, blanks, or periods may be used as delimiters between hours, minutes, and seconds. A period is required to separate seconds from fractional seconds.
- Data values must contain hours and minutes. Seconds and fractional seconds may be omitted.
- Data values may contain a sign.
- Hours may be of unlimited magnitude. The maximum for minutes is 59, and seconds must be less than 60 (for example, 59.99 is acceptable).

Internally, times are stored as the number of seconds.

Day and Time (DTIME). Time interval that includes days in the form ddd hh:mm:ss.ss. The following conventions apply:

- The number of days is separated from the hours by an acceptable Time delimiter: a blank, a period, or a colon. A preceding sign (+ or –) may be used.
- The maximum value for hours is 23.
- The remainder of the field must conform to required specifications for Time format. Fractional seconds must have the decimal indicator explicitly coded in the data value.

Day of Week (WKDAY). The day of the week expressed as a character string. Only the first two characters are significant. The remaining characters are optional. For example, Sunday can be expressed as Sunday, Sun, or Su. Internally, values are stored as integers from 1 to 7 (Sunday=1).

Month (MONTH). Month of the year expressed as an integer or a character string. Only the first three characters are significant. The remaining characters are optional. For example, January can be expressed as 1, January, or Jan. Internally, values are stored as integers from 1 to 12 (January=1).

Other Formats. Using SPSS syntax in a syntax window (see Chapter 4), you can specify different widths for many of the above formats, plus numerous other formats, including:

- Comma format: commas as thousands separators
- Dot format: Commas as decimal indicators and periods as thousands separators
- Scientific notation
- Percent
- Hexadecimal
- Column binary
- Packed decimal

For a complete list of data format types, see the *SPSS Base System Syntax Reference Guide*.

Value Assigned to Blanks for Numeric Variables. For fixed-format data, you can choose one of the following alternatives for the treatment of blank numeric fields:

○ **System missing.** Blank numeric fields are treated as missing data. This is the default.

○ **Value.** Blank numeric fields receive a user-specified value. For example, blanks may represent a value of 0 instead of missing data. Enter the value in the text box.

The following options are also available:

❏ **Display summary table.** Displays a summary table of defined variables, including data type and column location, in the output window.

❏ **Display warning message for undefined data.** If anything other than a number is encountered in a numeric field, the system-missing value is assigned, and a warning message is displayed in the output. To suppress the warning message, deselect this default setting.

Entering Variable Definitions

To enter a variable definition:

1. Specify the variable name, record and column locations, and data type.

2. Click on Add. The record number, start and end columns, variable name, and data type appear on the Defined Variables list, as shown in Figure 2.6.

Figure 2.6   Defined Variables

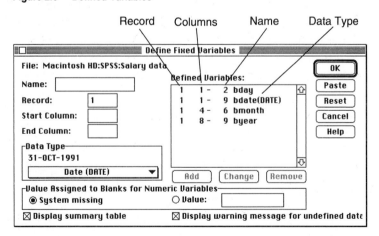

The following general rules apply:

• You can enter variables in any order. They are automatically sorted by record and start column on the list.

- You can specify multiple variables in the same or overlapping column locations. For example, in Figure 2.6, *bday* is in columns 1–2, *bmonth* in columns 4–6, *byear* in columns 8–9, and *bdate* in columns 1–9.

- You can read selective data fields and/or records. You don't have to define or read all the data in the file. SPSS reads only the columns and records you specify and skips over any data you don't define.

Changing and Deleting Variable Definitions

To change a variable definition, highlight the variable on the Defined Variables list, make the changes, and then click on Change. To delete a variable, highlight the variable on the Defined Variables list and click on Remove.

Define Freefield Variables

To define freefield format data, select Freefield for the File Format in the Read ASCII Data File dialog box and click on Define. This opens the Define Freefield Variables dialog box, as shown in Figure 2.7.

Figure 2.7   Define Freefield Variables dialog box

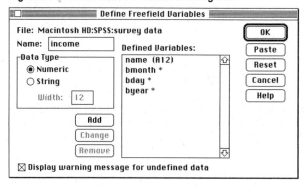

For each variable, you must specify the following:

Name. Variable names must begin with a letter and cannot exceed eight characters. Additional variable naming rules are given in "Define Fixed Variables" on p. 27.

Data Type. For freefield data, there are only two alternatives for data type:

- **Numeric.** Valid values include numbers, a leading plus or minus sign, and a decimal indicator. Imbedded thousands separators are not allowed in data values.

- **String.** Valid values include virtually any keyboard characters and imbedded blanks. For width, specify the *maximum* width of the string. Internally, shorter string values

are right-padded to the defined width. If the defined width is eight or fewer characters, it is a short string variable. If the defined width is more than eight characters, it
is a long string variable. Short string variables can be used in many SPSS procedures;
long string variables can be used in fewer procedures. If a value contains blanks, the
entire string must be enclosed in apostrophes or quotes.

The following option is also available:

❑ **Display warning message for undefined data.** If anything other than a number is encountered in a numeric field, the system-missing value is assigned, and a warning
message is displayed in the output. To suppress the warning message, deselect this
default setting.

Entering Variable Definitions

To enter a variable definition, specify the variable name and data type and click on Add.
The variable appears on the Defined Variables list. If it is a string variable, the letter A
and the defined width appear in parentheses next to the variable name.

While defining data in freefield format is relatively simple and easy, it is also easy to
make mistakes. Keep the following rules in mind:

- You must enter variables in the order in which they appear in the data file. Each new
  variable definition is added to the bottom of the list, and SPSS reads the variables in
  that order.

- You must provide definitions for all variables in the file. If you omit any, the data file
  will be read incorrectly. SPSS determines the end of one case and the beginning of
  the next based on the number of defined variables.

- The data file cannot contain any missing data. Blank fields are read as delimiters between variables, and SPSS does not distinguish between single and multiple blanks.
  If a single observation is missing, the entire remainder of the data file will be read
  incorrectly.

- If your Numbers control panel settings use a period as the decimal indicator, SPSS
  interprets commas as delimiters between values in freefield format. For example,
  a value of 1,234 is read as two separate values: 1 and 234.

Changing and Deleting Variable Definitions

To change a variable definition, highlight the variable on the Defined Variables list,
make the changes, and then click on Change. To delete a variable, highlight the variable
on the Defined Variables list and click on Remove.

Data Editor Window

When you open a data file, the data appear in the Data Editor window, as shown in Figure 2.8. You can then use the Data Editor to change variable definitions, add or delete cases or variables, and modify data values. For more information on the Data Editor, see Chapter 3.

Figure 2.8   Data Editor window

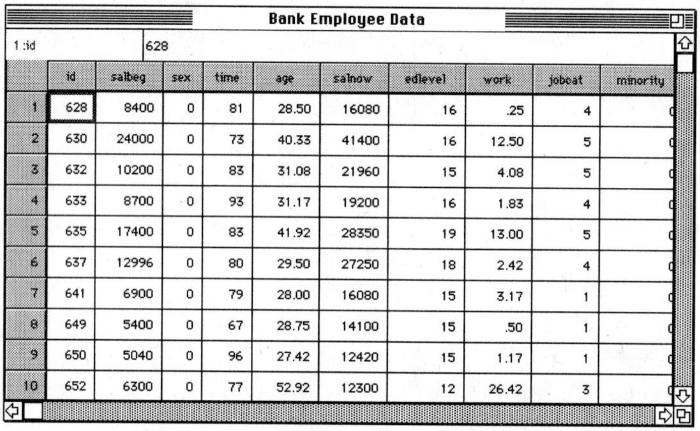

	id	salbeg	sex	time	age	salnow	edlevel	work	jobcat	minority
1	628	8400	0	81	28.50	16080	16	.25	4	
2	630	24000	0	73	40.33	41400	16	12.50	5	
3	632	10200	0	83	31.08	21960	15	4.08	5	
4	633	8700	0	93	31.17	19200	16	1.83	4	
5	635	17400	0	83	41.92	28350	19	13.00	5	
6	637	12996	0	80	29.50	27250	18	2.42	4	
7	641	6900	0	79	28.00	16080	15	3.17	1	
8	649	5400	0	67	28.75	14100	15	.50	1	
9	650	5040	0	96	27.42	12420	15	1.17	1	
10	652	6300	0	77	52.92	12300	12	26.42	3	

Bank Employee Data — 1 :id   628

File Information

An SPSS data file contains much more than raw data. It also contains any variable definition information, including:

• Variable names

• Variable formats

• Descriptive variable and value labels

This information is stored in the dictionary portion of the SPSS data file. The Data Editor provides one way to view the variable definition information (see Chapter 3). You can also display complete dictionary information for the working data file or any other SPSS data file.

Working Data File

To display complete dictionary information for every variable in the working data file, from the menus choose:

Utilities
  File Info

The following information is displayed in the output window:

- Variable names.
- Descriptive variable label (if any).
- Print and write formats. The data type is followed by a number indicating the maximum width and the number of decimal positions (if any). For example, F8.2 indicates a numeric variable with a maximum width of eight columns, including one column for the decimal indicator and two columns for decimal positions.
- Descriptive value labels (if any) for different values of the variable. Both the value and the corresponding label are displayed.

You can also obtain dictionary information on individual variables using the Variables dialog box (see Chapter 10).

Other SPSS Data Files

To display dictionary information in an output window for SPSS data files not currently open, from the menus choose:

File
  Display Data Info...

This opens a standard dialog box for selecting files. Select the file for which you want information.

Saving Data Files

Any changes you make in a data file last only until you close the data file—unless you explicitly save the changes. To save any changes to a previously defined SPSS data file:

1. Make the Data Editor the active window.

2. From the menus choose:

   File
     Save

The modified data file is saved, overwriting the previous version of the file.

Save As New File or Different Format

To save a new SPSS data file or save the data in a different file format:

1. Make the Data Editor the active window.

2. From the menus choose:

File
    Save As...

This opens a standard dialog box for saving files. Type or select a filename and a directory.

File Types

You can save data files in the following formats:

Save Data As. Select one of the following alternatives from the drop-down list:

◆ **SPSS data.** SPSS format. Data files saved in SPSS format can be read by compatible versions of SPSS (same version number or higher) on other operating systems.

SPSS portable data. Portable SPSS file that can be read by other versions of SPSS on other operating systems.

Tab-delimited data. ASCII text files with values separated by tabs.

Text. ASCII text file in fixed format, using the default write formats for all variables. There are no tabs or spaces between variable fields.

Microsoft Excel. Microsoft Excel spreadsheet file. The maximum number of variables is 256.

Lotus 1-2-3 Release 3.0. Lotus 1-2-3 spreadsheet file, release 3.0. The maximum number of variables you can save is 256.

Lotus 1-2-3 Release 2.0. Lotus 1-2-3 spreadsheet file, release 2.0. The maximum number of variables you can save is 256.

Lotus 1-2-3 Release 1.0. Lotus 1-2-3 spreadsheet file, release 1.0. The maximum number of variables you can save is 256.

SYLK. Symbolic link format for Microsoft Excel and Multiplan spreadsheet files. The maximum number of variables you can save is 256.

dBASE IV. dBASE IV-format files. The maximum number of variables you can save is 255.

dBASE III. dBASE III-format files. The maximum number of variables you can save is 128.

dBASE II. dBASE II-format files. The maximum number of variables you can save is 32.

For SPSS data files, the following option is available:

❑ **Compress SPSS data.** Compressed files occupy less disk space and usually take less time to process than uncompressed files.

For Lotus 1-2-3, Excel, SYLK, and tab-delimited files, the following option is available:

❑ **Write variable names to spreadsheet.** Variable names are written in the first row of the file.

If you save as SPSS format, the new file becomes the working data file and the new file-name is displayed on the title bar of the Data Editor window. If you save as any other format, the working data file is unaffected.

Closing a Data File

Since only one data file can be open at a time, SPSS automatically closes the working data file before it opens another one. If there have been any changes to the data file since it was last saved, SPSS asks if you want to save the changes before it closes the file and opens the next one.

3 Data Editor

The Data Editor provides a convenient, spreadsheet-like method for creating and editing SPSS data files. The Data Editor window, shown in Figure 3.1, opens automatically when you start an SPSS session.

Figure 3.1   Data Editor window

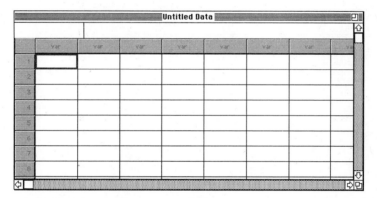

If you have previous experience with spreadsheet programs, many of the features of the Data Editor should be familiar. There are, however, several important distinctions.

- **Rows are cases**. Each row represents a **case** or an observation. For example, each individual respondent to a questionnaire is a case.

- **Columns are variables**. Each column represents a **variable** or characteristic being measured. For example, each item on a questionnaire is a variable.

- **Cells contain values**. Each cell contains a single value of a variable for a case. The cell is the intersection of the case and variable. Cells contain only data values. Unlike spreadsheet programs, cells in the Data Editor cannot contain formulas.

- **The data file is rectangular**. The dimensions of the data file are determined by the number of cases and variables. You can enter data in any cell. If you enter data in a cell outside the boundaries of the defined data file, SPSS extends the data rectangle to include any rows and/or columns between that cell and the file boundaries. There are no "empty" cells within the boundaries of the data file. For numeric variables, blank cells are converted to the system-missing value (see "Missing Values" on p. 45). For string variables, a blank is considered a valid value.

Defining Variables

When you open an existing data file (see Chapter 2), the data are displayed in the Data Editor, as shown in Figure 3.2. Any existing data definition recognized by SPSS (that is, variable names, formats, etc.) is reflected in the display. Beyond the boundaries of the defined data file, the Data Editor displays dimmed row numbers and dimmed column headings to indicate potential cases and variables.

Figure 3.2   Data file displayed in the Data Editor

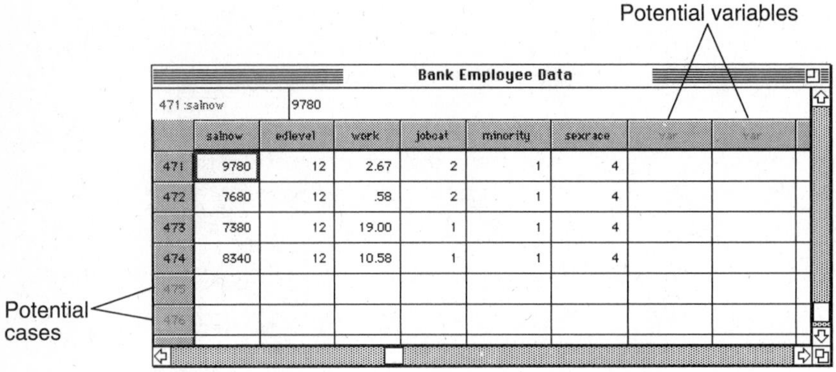

You can replace existing or default data definitions with your own specifications. You can:

- Create your own variable names.
- Provide descriptive variable and value labels.
- Use special codes for missing values.
- Assign different formats (such as string, date, and time).

To change the name, format, and other attributes of a variable:

- Double-click on the current variable name at the top of the column

or

- Select any cell in the column for the variable, and from the menus choose:

Data
  Define Variable...

This opens the Define Variable dialog box, as shown in Figure 3.3.

Figure 3.3   Define Variable dialog box

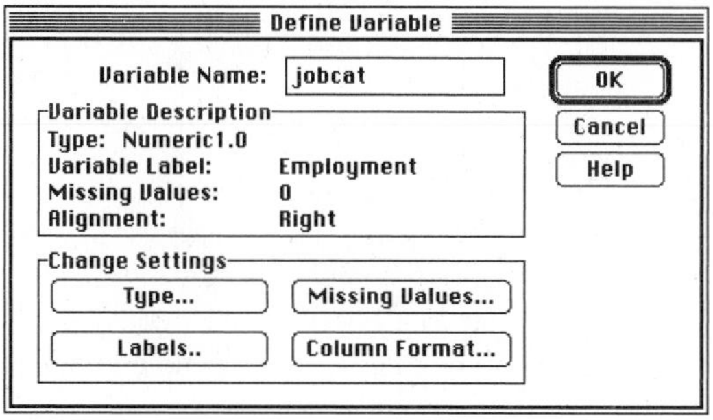

The variable name, type, label, missing values (if any), and alignment for the selected variable are displayed.

Variable Names

The default name for new variables is the prefix *var* and a sequential five-digit number (*var00001*, *var00002*, etc.). To change the variable name, simply enter a new name of up to eight characters in the Variable Name text box. For further information on rules for naming variables, consult the Help system.

Renamed Variables in Dialog Boxes

Source variable lists in dialog boxes are updated to reflect new variable names, but, in some cases, selected variable lists may not be updated. If a selected variable list contains an old variable name and you want to run the procedure again during the same session, you should remove the variable name from the selected variable list or an error will result.

To remove an old variable name from a selected variable list, select the variable and click on the ◄ pushbutton. This removes the variable name without placing it back on the source variable list.

Variable Type

By default, SPSS assumes that all new variables are numeric. To change the variable type, click on Type in the Define Variable dialog box. This opens the Define Variable Type dialog box, as shown in Figure 3.4.

Figure 3.4   Define Variable Type dialog box

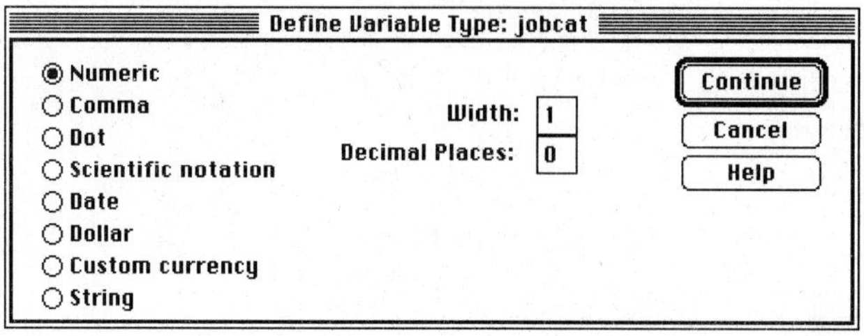

The contents of the Define Variable Type dialog box depend on the data type selected. The available data types are:

○ **Numeric**. Values are numbers, and a period (.) is the decimal indicator.

○ **Comma**. Values are numbers, commas are used as thousands separators, and a period is the decimal indicator.

○ **Dot**. Values are numbers, periods are used as thousands separators, and a comma is the decimal indicator.

○ **Scientific notation**. Values are numbers expressed in scientific notation.

○ **Dollar**. Values are numbers with a leading dollar sign ($).

○ **Custom currency**. Values are numbers in custom currency format. See Chapter 11 for information about defining custom currency formats.

○ **String**. Values are alphanumeric strings.

For some data types, there are text boxes for width and number of decimals; for others, you can simply select a format from a scrollable list of examples. For detailed descriptions of variable types and valid values, consult the Help system.

SPSS data files created on other operating systems or generated by command syntax in a syntax window may contain other data formats. If the selected variable uses one of these other formats, the format appears as an additional alternative at the bottom of the list. You can change the format to one of the standard format alternatives—but once you apply the change, you cannot change the variable back to its original format. Other formats recognized by SPSS include:

• Implied decimal

• Percent

• Hexadecimal

• Column binary

Input versus Display Formats

Depending on the format, the display of values in the Data Editor may differ from the actual value as entered and stored internally. Here are some general guidelines:

- For numeric, comma, and dot formats, you can enter values with any number of decimal positions (up to 16), and the entire value is stored internally. The Data Editor displays only the defined number of decimal places, and it rounds values with more decimals. However, the complete value is used in any computations.

- For string variables, all values are right-padded to the maximum width. For a string variable with a width of 6, a value of 'No' is stored internally as 'No   ' and is not equivalent to ' No '.

- For date formats, you can use slashes, dashes, spaces, commas, or periods as delimiters between day, month, and year values, and you can enter numbers, three-letter abbreviations, or complete names for month values. Dates of the general format dd-mmm-yy are displayed with dashes as delimiters and three-letter abbreviations for the month. Dates of the general format dd/mm/yy and mm/dd/yy are displayed with slashes for delimiters and numbers for the month. Internally, dates are stored as the number of seconds from October 14, 1582.

- For time formats, you can use colons, periods, or spaces as delimiters between hours, minutes, and seconds. Times are displayed with colons as delimiters. Internally, times are stored as the number of seconds.

See the *SPSS Base System Syntax Reference Guide* for more information about input and display data formats.

Decimal Indicators and Numbers Control Panel Settings

For numeric format variables, the decimal indicator can be either a period or a comma, depending on the setting in the Numbers control panel. If the decimal indicator is anything other than a period, SPSS uses a comma as the decimal indicator. Comma, dollar, dot, and custom currency formats are not affected by the decimal indicator setting.

Labels

To provide descriptive variable and value labels, click on Labels in the Define Variable dialog box. This opens the Define Labels dialog box, as shown in Figure 3.5.

Figure 3.5   Define Labels dialog box

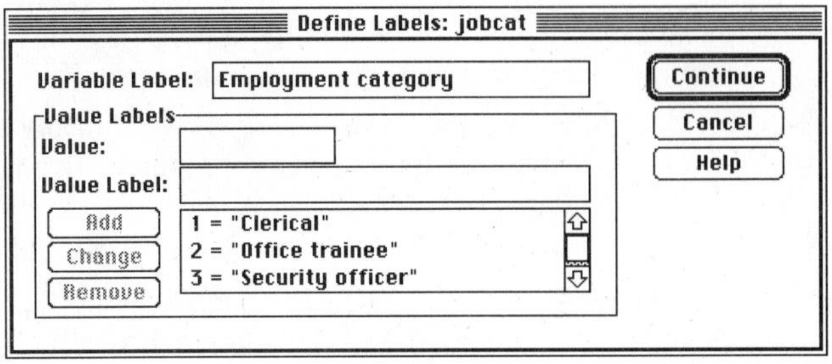

Variable Label

Variable labels can be up to 120 characters long, although most procedures display fewer than 120 characters in output. Variable labels are case sensitive; they are displayed exactly as entered.

Value Labels

You can assign a label for each value of a variable. This is particularly useful if your data file uses numeric codes to represent non-numeric categories (for example, codes of 1 and 2 for male and female). Value labels can be up to 60 characters long, although most procedures display fewer than 60 characters in output. Value labels are case sensitive; they are displayed exactly as entered. Value labels are not available for long string variables.

Assigning a label. To assign value labels:

1. Enter the value in the Value text box. The value can be numeric or string.

2. Enter a label in the Value Label text box.

3. Click on Add. The value label is added to the list.

Modifying a label. To modify a value label:

1. Highlight the label on the list.

2. Enter the new label (or value) in the text box.

3. Click on Change. The new label appears on the list.

Deleting a label. To delete a value label:

1. Highlight the value label.

2. Click on Remove. The label is removed from the list.

You can display value labels instead of values in the Data Editor window. You can also use value label lists for data entry. (See "Display Value Labels" on p. 59.)

Missing Values

In SPSS, there are two types of missing values:

- **System-missing values**. Any blank numeric cells in the data rectangle are assigned the system-missing value, which is indicated with a period (.).

- **User-missing values**. It is often useful to be able to distinguish why information is missing. You can assign values that identify information missing for specific reasons and then instruct SPSS to flag these values as missing. SPSS statistical procedures and data transformations recognize this flag, and those cases with user-missing values are handled specially. Figure 3.6 shows how user-missing values are treated by the Frequencies procedure.

Figure 3.6   User-missing values

```
OZONE      Concern About Ozone Depletion


                                          Valid     Cum
Value Label                Value Frequency Percent  Percent  Percent

Very concerned              1.00     237    51.3    54.4     54.4
Somewhat concerned          2.00     144    31.2    33.0     87.4
Not concerned               3.00      55    11.9    12.6    100.0
Never use ozone             8.00       9     1.9   Missing
No answer                   9.00      17     3.7   Missing

                          Total      462   100.0   100.0

Valid cases      436    Missing cases      26
```

User-missing values

User-Missing Values

To specify user-missing values, click on Missing Values in the Define Variable dialog box. This opens the Define Missing Values dialog box, as shown in Figure 3.7.

Figure 3.7   Define Missing Values dialog box

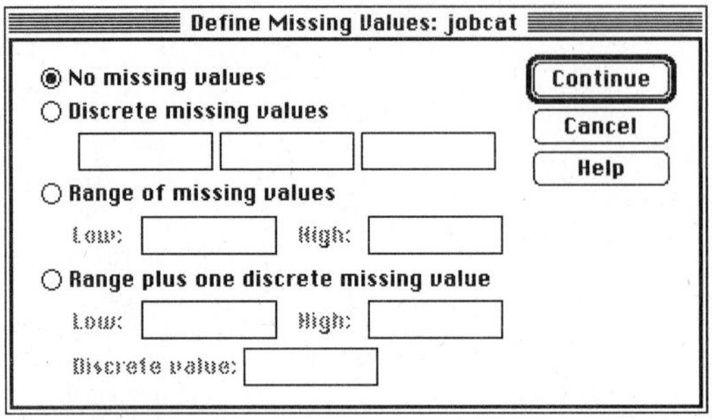

User-missing values can be assigned to variables of any format type except long string (see "Variable Type" on p. 41). You can choose one of the following alternatives:

○ **No missing values**. No user-missing values. All values are treated as valid. This is the default.

○ **Discrete missing values**. You can enter up to three discrete (individual) user-missing values for a variable. You can define discrete missing values for numeric or short string variables.

○ **Range of missing values**. All values between and including the low and high values are flagged as missing. Not available for short string variables.

○ **Range plus one discrete missing value**. All values between the low and high values and one additional value outside the range are flagged as missing. Not available for short string variables.

If you want to include all values below or above a certain value in a range but you don't know what the lowest or highest possible value is, you can enter an asterisk (*) for **Low** or **High**.

Column Format

To adjust the width of the Data Editor columns or to change the alignment of data in the column, click on Column Format in the Define Variable dialog box. This opens the Define Column Format dialog box, as shown in Figure 3.8.

Figure 3.8   Define Column Format dialog box

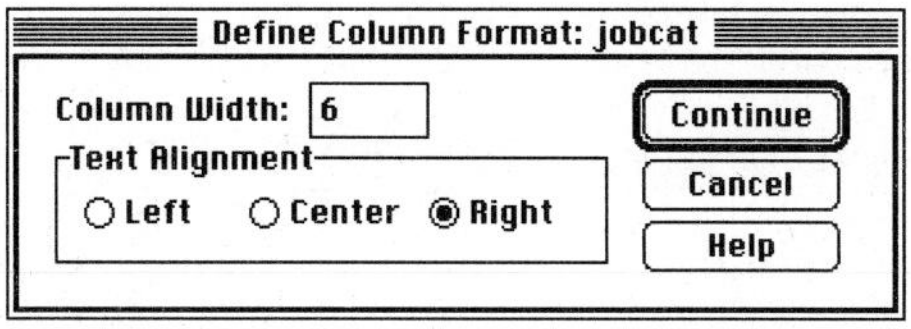

Column Width. The default column width is determined by the defined width of the variable (see "Variable Type" on p. 41). To change the column width, enter a new value. You can also change the column width in the Data Editor window. Position the mouse pointer on the border between two variable names at the top of the Data Editor window and use the click-and-drag technique to move the column border.

New column widths remain in effect as long as the data file is open or until they are changed again. They are not saved with the data file. The next time you open the file, the default column widths are used.

Text Alignment. The default alignment depends on the data type. You can choose one of the following alternatives:

○ **Left.** Text is left-aligned. This is the default for string variables.

○ **Center.** Text is centered.

○ **Right.** Text is right-aligned. This is the default for nonstring variables.

Column Width versus Variable Width

Column formats affect only the display of values in the Data Editor. Changing the column width does not change the defined width of a variable. If the defined and actual width of a value are wider than the column, the value appears truncated in the Data Editor window.

Templates

You can assign the same variable definition information to multiple variables with variable templates. For example, if you have a group of variables that all use the numeric codes 1 and 2 to represent "yes" and "no" responses and 9 to represent missing responses, you can create a template that contains those value labels and missing value specifications and apply the template to the entire group of variables.

To create, apply, or modify a template, from the menus choose:

Data
  Templates...

This opens the Template dialog box, as shown in Figure 3.9.

Figure 3.9   Template dialog box

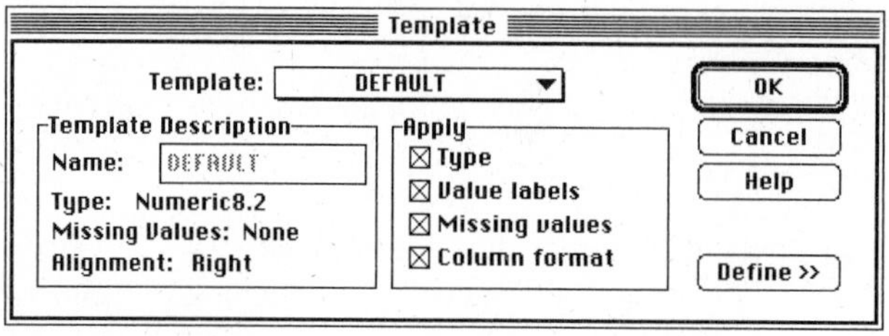

You can select and apply one of the existing templates from the Template list, modify it, or create a new template.

Applying Templates

To apply an existing template, select a template from the list and specify the template characteristics to be applied.

→ **Template**. All of the existing templates are listed. The description of the most recently selected template is displayed. SPSS comes with the following predefined templates:

Default. Numeric, eight characters wide, two decimal positions.

Months. A numeric variable with the month names as value labels for the values 1 through 12.

States. A two-character string variable with the full state names as value labels for the corresponding two-character zip code abbreviation.

Weekdays. A numeric variable with the weekday names as value labels for the values 1 through 7.

Template Description. The currently selected template name, variable type, user-missing values, and alignment are displayed.

Apply. You can apply any or all of the template characteristics to the selected variables. Choose one or more of the following alternatives:

❑ **Type**. Variable type (for example, numeric, string, or date).

❑ **Value labels**. Descriptive labels for value categories (for example, labels of *No* and *Yes* for values coded 0 and 1).

❑ **Missing values**. User-missing values (see "Missing Values" on p. 45).

❑ **Column format**. Column width and alignment for display in the Data Editor (see "Column Format" on p. 46).

Creating and Modifying Templates

To modify an existing template or to create a new one, click on Define>>. This expands the Template dialog box, as shown in Figure 3.10.

Figure 3.10   Expanded Template dialog box

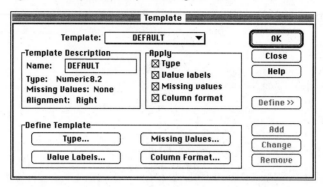

Defining a template is almost identical to defining a variable and uses the same dialog boxes for variable type, labels, missing values, and column format (see "Variable Type" on p. 41 through "Column Format" on p. 46).

Modify a template. To modify an existing template:

1. Select the template from the Template list.

2. Make the changes using the Define Template options.

3. Click on Change.

4. Click on OK to apply the template to the selected variables or click on Close to save the modified template without applying it to any variables. Any variables defined with the template but not currently selected remain unchanged.

Create a new template. To create a new template:

1. Select an existing template from the Template list. (If possible, select a template similar to the one you want to create.)

2. Use the Define Template options to create the template.

3. Enter a name for the template in the Name text box.

4. Click on Add.

5. Click on OK to apply the template to the selected variables or click on Close to save the modified template without applying it to any variables.

Entering Data

You can enter data in virtually any order. You can enter data by case or by variable, for selected areas or individual cells. To enter a value in a cell:

1. Click on the cell or use the arrow keys to move to the cell. As shown in Figure 3.11, a heavy border appears around the cell, indicating that it is the active cell. The variable name and the row number are displayed in the upper left corner of the Data Editor window.
2. Type in the value. The value is displayed in the cell editor at the top of the Data Editor window. (See "Data Value Restrictions" on p. 51 for data value restrictions.)
3. Press ↵Return (or select another cell). The data value from the cell editor appears in the cell.

If you select a single cell, the ↵Return and Tab⇥ keys move down and right one cell, respectively. ⇧Shift-Tab⇥ moves left one cell. If you enter a value in a column outside the boundaries of the defined data file, you automatically create a new variable. If you enter a value in a row outside the boundaries of the data file, you automatically create a new case.

Figure 3.11 Active cell and cell editor

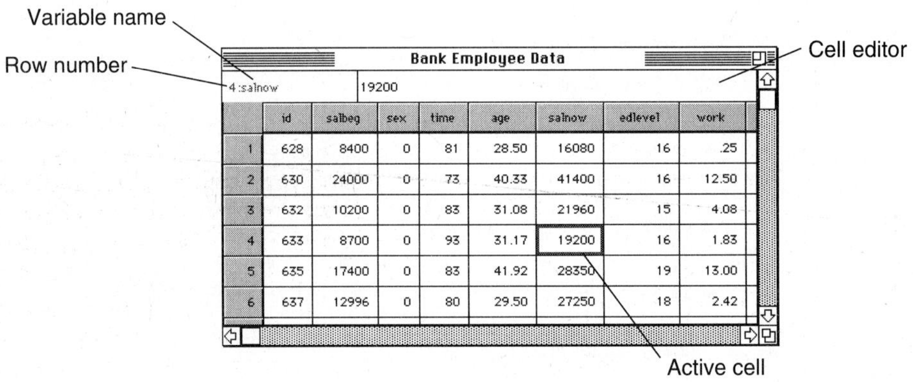
Variable name
Row number
Cell editor
Active cell
Bank Employee Data
4:salnow
19200
id salbeg sex time age salnow edlevel work
1 628 8400 0 81 28.50 16080 16 .25
2 630 24000 0 73 40.33 41400 16 12.50
3 632 10200 0 83 31.08 21960 15 4.08
4 633 8700 0 93 31.17 19200 16 1.83
5 635 17400 0 83 41.92 28350 19 13.00
6 637 12996 0 80 29.50 27250 18 2.42

Entering Data in a Selected Area

You can restrict and control the flow of movement by selecting an area for data entry.

- **Select a case (row).** Click on the case number on the left side of the row. This highlights the entire row. Both the ↵Return and Tab⇥ keys are restricted to movement between variables (columns) for that case.

- **Select a variable (column)**. Click on the variable name at the top of the column. This highlights the entire column. Both the ⏎Return and Tab→ keys are restricted to movement between cases for that variable.

- **Select an area of cases and variables**. Click and drag the mouse diagonally from one corner of the area to the far corner (for example, upper left to lower right). The Tab→ key moves from left to right through the variables for each case in the selected area. The ⏎Return key moves from top to bottom through the cases for each variable in the selected area. (See Figure 3.12.)

Figure 3.12   Moving in a selected area

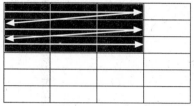
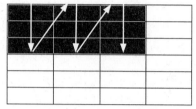

Tab key movement   Return key movement

Data Value Restrictions

The defined variable type and width determine the type of value that can be entered in the cell.

- If you type a character not allowed by the defined variable type, the Data Editor beeps and does not enter the character.

- For string variables, characters beyond the defined width are not allowed.

- For numeric variables, integer values that exceed the defined width can be entered, but the Data Editor displays either scientific notation or asterisks in the cell to indicate that the value is wider than the defined width. To display the value in the cell, change the defined width of the variable. (*Note*: Changing the *column* width does not affect the *variable* width.)

Editing Data

With the Data Editor, you can modify a data file in many ways. You can:

- Change data values.
- Cut, copy, and paste data values.
- Add and delete cases.
- Add and delete variables.

- Change the order of variables.
- Change variable definitions.

Changing Data Values

To change a data value, you can either replace the entire value or modify part of it.

Replace a value. To delete the old value and enter a new value:

1. Click on the cell or use the arrow keys to move to the cell. The cell value is displayed in the cell editor.

2. Enter the new value. It replaces the old value in the cell editor.

3. Press ⏎Return (or select another cell). The new value appears in the cell.

Modify a value. To modify a data value using the mouse:

1. Click on the cell. The cell value appears in the cell editor.

2. Click on the cell editor. A blinking cursor appears at the position where you clicked the mouse. To reposition the cursor, simply aim and click the mouse again.

3. Edit the data value as you would any other text (see Chapter 4).

4. Press ⏎Return (or select another cell). The modified value appears in the cell.

Cutting, Copying, and Pasting Values

You can cut, copy, and paste individual cell values or groups of values. You can:
- Move or copy a single cell value to another cell.
- Move or copy a single cell value to a group of cells.
- Move or copy the values for a single case (row) to multiple cases.
- Move or copy the values for a single variable (column) to multiple variables.
- Move or copy a group of cell values to another group of cells.

Move or Copy Cell Values

To move or copy cell values:

1. Select the cell value(s) you want to cut or copy.

2. From the menus choose:

    Edit
      Cut

    or

    Edit
      Copy

3. Select the target cell(s).

4. From the menus choose:

    Edit
      Paste

The pasted values appear in the cells, unless the defined variable types are not the same and no conversion is possible.

Data Conversion

If the defined variable types of the source and target cells are not the same, SPSS attempts to convert the value. If no conversion is possible, SPSS inserts the system-missing value in the target cell.

- **Numeric or Date into String**. Numeric (for example, numeric, dollar, dot, or comma) and date formats are converted to strings if they are pasted into a string variable cell. The string value is the numeric value displayed in the cell. For example, for a dollar format variable, the displayed dollar sign becomes part of the string value. Values that exceed the defined string variable width are truncated.

- **String into Numeric or Date**. String values that contain acceptable characters for the numeric or date format of the target cell are converted to the equivalent numeric or date value. For example, a string value of 25/12/91 is converted to a valid date if the format type of the target cell is one of the day-month-year formats, but it is converted to system-missing if the format type of the target cell is one of the month-day-year formats.

- **Date into Numeric**. Date and time values are converted to a number of seconds if the target cell is one of the numeric formats (for example, numeric, dollar, dot, or comma). Since dates are stored internally as the number of seconds since October 14, 1582, converting dates to numeric values can yield some extremely large numbers. For example, the date 10/29/91 is converted to a numeric value of 12,908,073,600.

- **Numeric into Date or Time**. Numeric values are converted to dates or times if the value represents a number of seconds that can produce a valid date or time. For dates, numeric values less than 86,400 are converted to the system-missing value.

Pasting into Areas with Different Dimensions

If the target area does not have the same number of rows and columns as the source area, the pasting rules shown in Figure 3.13 apply.

Figure 3.13   Pasting into areas with different dimensions

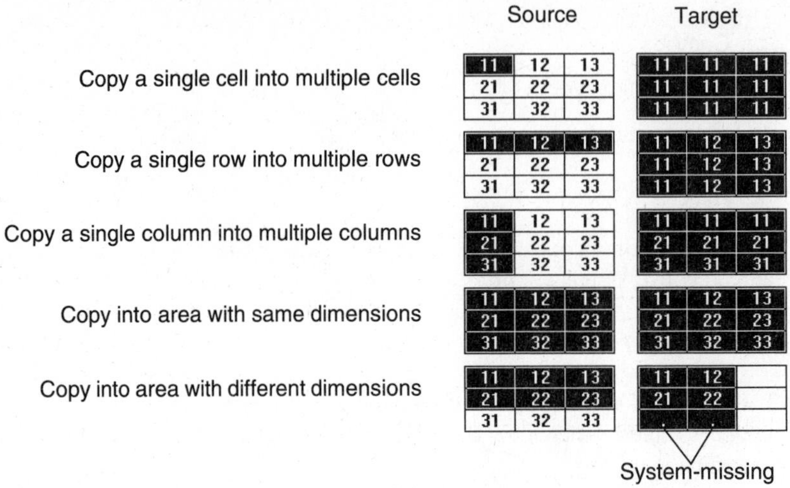

	Source	Target

Copy a single cell into multiple cells

11	12	13		11	11	11
21	22	23		11	11	11
31	32	33		11	11	11

Copy a single row into multiple rows

11	12	13		11	12	13
21	22	23		11	12	13
31	32	33		11	12	13

Copy a single column into multiple columns

11	12	13		11	11	11
21	22	23		21	21	21
31	32	33		31	31	31

Copy into area with same dimensions

11	12	13		11	12	13
21	22	23		21	22	23
31	32	33		31	32	33

Copy into area with different dimensions

11	12	13		11	12	
21	22	23		21	22	
31	32	33				

System-missing

Pasting Outside the Defined Data File

If you paste values outside the boundaries of the defined data file, SPSS extends the data file to include the pasted area and creates new cases and/or new variables as needed with system-missing values for new cells outside the pasted area (see Figure 3.14).

Figure 3.14   Pasting outside the defined data file

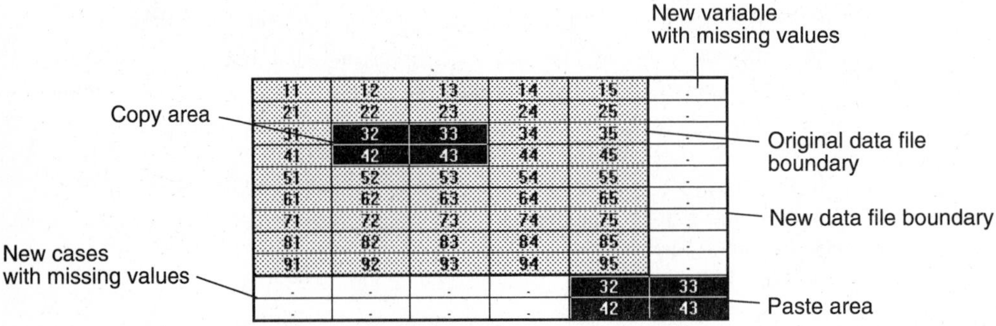

Pasting Outside the Data Editor

You can paste data from the Data Editor into a syntax or an output window or into another application. If you paste data values outside the Data Editor, what you see displayed in the cell is what is pasted. For example, if the real value of a cell is 1.29 but it is displayed as 1.3, the value 1.3 is pasted. If you display value labels instead of values (see "Display Value Labels" on p. 59), the value labels are pasted, not the actual values.

Inserting New Cases

Entering data in a cell on a blank row automatically creates a new case. SPSS inserts the system-missing value for all the other variables for that case. If there are any blank rows between the new case and the existing cases, the blank rows also become new cases with the system-missing value for all variables.

Insert a new case between existing cases. To insert a new case between existing cases:

1. Select any cell in the case (row) below the position where you want to insert the new case.

2. From the menus choose:

   Data
    Insert Case

 or click on the Insert Case tool. A new row is inserted for the case and all variables receive the system-missing value.

Inserting New Variables

Entering data in a blank column automatically creates a new variable with a default variable name (the prefix *var* and a sequential five-digit number) and a default data format type (numeric). SPSS inserts the system-missing value for all cases for the new variable. If there are any blank columns between the new variable and the existing variables, these columns also become new variables with the system-missing value for all cases.

Insert a new variable between existing variables. To insert a new variable between existing variables:

1. Select any cell in the variable (column) to the right of the position where you want to insert the new variable.

2. From the menus choose:

   Data
    Insert Variable

 or click on the Insert Variable tool. A new variable is inserted with the system-missing value for all cases.

Deleting Cases and Variables

Delete a case. To delete a case (row):

1. Click on the case number on the left side of the row. The entire row is highlighted. To delete multiple cases, use the click-and-drag method to extend the selection.

2. From the menus choose:

   Edit
     Clear

The selected cases are deleted. Any cases below them shift up.

Delete a variable. To delete a variable (column):

1. Click on the variable name at the top of the column or select any cell in the column. The entire column is highlighted.

   To delete multiple variables, use the click-and-drag method to extend the selection.

2. From the menus choose:

   Edit
     Clear

The selected variables are deleted. Any variables to the right of the deleted variables shift to the left.

Deleted Variables in Dialog Boxes

Source variable lists in dialog boxes are updated when variables are deleted, but, in some cases, selected variable lists may not be updated. If a selected variable list contains a deleted variable and you want to run the procedure again during the same session, you should remove the variable name from the selected variable list or an error will result.

To remove a deleted variable name from a selected variable list, select the variable and click on the ◀ pushbutton. This removes the variable name without placing it back on the source variable list.

Moving Variables

To move a variable by cutting and pasting in the Data Editor:

1. Insert a new variable in the position where you want to move the existing variable (see "Inserting New Variables" on p. 55).

2. For the variable you want to move, click on the variable name at the top of the column. The entire column is highlighted.

3. From the menus choose:

    Edit
      Cut

    The selected variable is cut. Any variables to the right of the cut variables shift to the left.

4. Click on the variable name of the new, inserted variable. The entire variable is highlighted.

5. From the menus choose:

    Edit
      Paste

    The cut variable is pasted into the new variable space. All dictionary information for the variable is retained.

Changing Data Type

You can change the data type for a variable at any time using the Define Variable Type dialog box (see "Variable Type" on p. 41), and SPSS will attempt to convert existing values to the new type. If no conversion is possible, SPSS assigns the system-missing value. The conversion rules are the same as those for pasting data values to a variable with a different format type (see "Cutting, Copying, and Pasting Values" on p. 52). If the change in data format may result in the loss of missing value specifications or value labels, SPSS displays an alert box and asks if you want to proceed with the change or cancel it.

Finding Variables

Because variables are not always sorted in alphabetical order, it can sometimes be difficult to find a specific variable, particularly if the data file contains a large number of variables. You can use the Go To pushbutton in the Variables dialog box to find the selected variable in the Data Editor window. For more information about the Variables dialog box, see Chapter 10.

Finding Cases

To find a specific case (row) in the Data Editor, from the menus choose:

Data
  Go To Case...

This opens the Go to Case dialog box, as shown in Figure 3.15.

Figure 3.15   Go to Case dialog box

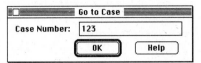

For Case Number, enter the row number for the case in the Data Editor. This value re-flects the current position of the case in the data file. It is not a fixed value of a case ID variable. If you change the position of the case by inserting or deleting cases above it or by sorting the data file, the case number value changes.

Finding Data Values

Within a variable, you can search for specific data values or value labels in the Data Ed-itor. To search for a data value:

1. Select any cell in the column of the variable you want to search.

2. From the menus choose:

    Edit
      Search for Data...

This opens the Search for Data dialog box, as shown in Figure 3.16.

Figure 3.16   Search for Data dialog box

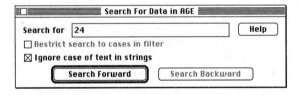

You can search forward or backward from the active cell location. To search for a value label, value labels must be turned on (see "Display Value Labels" on p. 59).

The following options are also available:

❏ **Restrict search to cases in filter.** If you have selected a subset of cases but have not dis-carded unselected cases, you can restrict the data search to only the subset by select-ing this option.

❏ **Ignore case of text in strings**. By default, the search for string values in string variables and value labels ignores case. Deselect this default setting for a case-sensitive search.

Case Selection Status

If you have selected a subset of cases but have not discarded unselected cases, unselected cases are marked in the Data Editor with a diagonal line through the row number, as shown in Figure 3.17.

Figure 3.17   Selection filter status

Unselected
(excluded)
cases

	id	salbeg	sex	time	age	salnow	edlevel	work	jobcat	minority
1	628	8400	0	81	28.50	16080	16	.25	4	0
2	630	24000	0	73	40.33	41400	16	12.50	5	0
3	632	10200	0	83	31.08	21960	15	4.08	5	0
4	633	8700	0	93	31.17	19200	16	1.83	4	0
5	635	17400	0	83	41.92	28350	19	13.00	5	0
6	637	12996	0	80	29.50	27250	18	2.42	4	0
7	641	6900	0	79	28.00	16080	15	3.17	1	0
8	649	5400	0	67	28.75	14100	15	.50	1	0
9	650	5040	0	96	27.42	12420	15	1.17	1	0
10	652	6300	0	77	52.92	12300	12	26.42	3	0

Bank Employee Data

1 :id   628

Preferences

The Utilities menu offers several additional features to customize the Data Editor. You can:

- Display value labels instead of values.
- Control the automatic creation of new cases.
- Turn the grid lines on and off for display and/or printing.
- Change fonts for display and/or printing.

Display Value Labels

If you have defined descriptive value labels for any variables, you can display these labels in the Data Editor instead of the actual values. From the menus choose:

Utilities
  Value Labels

 or click on the Value Labels tool.

Data Entry with Value Labels

The Value Labels option also provides a list of value labels for data entry, as shown in Figure 3.18. To use the value label list for data entry:

1. Use the mouse or the arrow keys to select the cell. The actual value (not the label) is displayed in the cell editor.

2. Option-click the mouse button to display the list of value labels for that variable. If value labels have not been defined for the variable, no list appears.

3. Select the value label you want to enter from the list.

Figure 3.18   Data entry with value labels

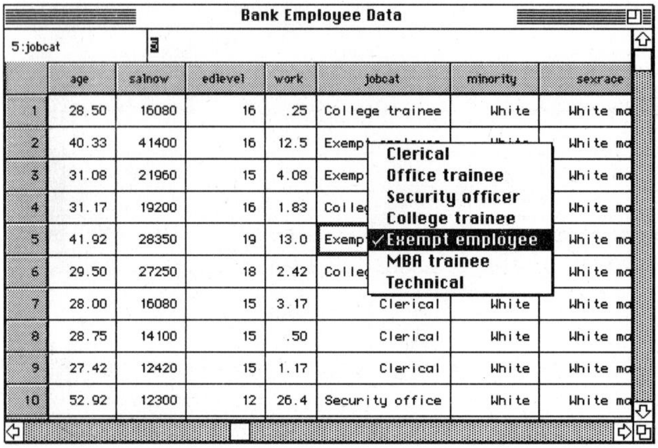

Auto New Case

By default, a new case is automatically created if you move down a row from the last defined case by pressing the ⏎Return key. To turn this feature on and off, from the menus choose:

Utilities
  Auto New Case

Grid Lines

You can turn the Data Editor grid lines on and off for both display and printing. From the menus choose:

Utilities
  Grid Lines

Fonts

To change the font in which data values are displayed and printed, from the menus choose:

Utilities
  Fonts...

This opens the Fonts dialog box. Select a font, size, and style. Font changes are applied to all of the data values in the Data Editor window. Fonts cannot be selectively applied to portions of the data. See Chapter 10 for more information.

Printing

To print the contents of the Data Editor:

1. Make the Data Editor the active window.

2. From the menus choose:

    File
      Print...

This opens the Print dialog box. For more information about printing, see Chapter 9.

Pending Transformations and the Data Editor

If you have pending transformations (see Chapter 11), the following limitations apply to the Data Editor:

- Variables cannot be inserted or deleted.
- Variable names and format type cannot be changed.
- Variables cannot be reordered.
- Templates cannot be applied to potential variables.
- If you change any data values, the changes may be overwritten when the transformations are executed. An alert box asks if you want to run the pending transformations.

Saving Data Files

Any changes you make to a data file in the Data Editor window last only for the duration of the SPSS session or until you open another data file—unless you explicitly save the changes. To save a previously defined SPSS data file:

1. Make the Data Editor the active window.

2. From the menus choose:

   File
     Save

The modified data file is saved, overwriting the previous version of the file.

Save As New File or Different Format

To save a new SPSS data file or to save the data in a different file format:

1. Make the Data Editor the active window.

2. From the menus choose:

   File
     Save As...

This opens a standard dialog box for saving files. See Chapter 2 for more information on saving data files.

Closing a Data File and Opening a Different One

Only one data file can be open at any time. If you have an open data file and then open a different one, SPSS automatically closes the open data file first. If there have been any changes to the data file since it was last saved, SPSS asks if you want to save the changes before it closes the file and opens the next one.

4 Output and Syntax Windows

In SPSS, there are two types of text windows:

Output windows. The text-based results of your SPSS session are displayed in output windows. This includes any nongraphic statistical results, such as a crosstabulation or a correlation matrix.

Syntax windows. Syntax windows are text windows that you can use to run SPSS commands with command syntax. You can generate SPSS command syntax by pasting your dialog box choices into a syntax window. You can then edit the command syntax to take advantage of features not available in the dialog box interface. You can save the commands in text files and run them again in other SPSS sessions. If you have existing command files, you can open these in a syntax window and run the commands.

You can open any text file in an output or a syntax window. However, output generated during the session is always displayed in an output window, and you can run command syntax only from a syntax window.

Output Windows

An output window opens automatically when you start an SPSS session. You can have more than one open output window. These windows can contain new or existing output or text files.

Opening a New Output Window

To open a new output window, from the menus choose:

File
  New...

This opens a dialog box for selecting a file type. Select SPSS Output and click on Open. This opens a new output window.

Opening an Existing Output File

To open an existing output or text file in an output window, from the menus choose:

File
  Open...

This opens a standard dialog box for selecting files. The file can be a previously saved SPSS output or syntax file or a file created in another application and saved in text format. The file is displayed in a new output window.

Multiple Output Windows

If you have more than one output window open, SPSS sends output results to the **designated output window**. Although you can open multiple output windows, there can be only one designated output window. By default, the output window that opens automatically at the start of the session is the designated output window.

To designate a different output window, make the output window the active window and click on the Designate Window tool on the toolbar or choose Designate Window from the Utilities menu.

All new output is appended to the bottom of the file in the designated output window. The window remains the designated output window until you select another. You cannot close the designated output window. There is always at least one open output window in an SPSS session.

Syntax Windows

The dialog box interface is designed to handle most of the capabilities of SPSS. Underlying the dialog boxes, there is a command language that you can use to access additional features and customize your analysis. After you make your dialog box selections, you can use the Paste pushbutton to paste this underlying command syntax into a syntax window. You can then edit the resulting text and run the modified commands from the syntax window (see "Using SPSS Command Syntax in a Syntax Window" on p. 65).

Opening a New Text File in a Syntax Window

If you don't have an open syntax window, one opens automatically the first time you use the Paste pushbutton. You can also use the menus to open a new text file in a syntax window. From the menus choose:

File
  New...

This opens a dialog box for selecting a file type. Select SPSS Syntax and click on Open. This opens a syntax window for a new text file.

Opening an Existing File in a Syntax Window

To open an existing text file in a syntax window, from the menus choose:

File
  Open...

This opens a standard dialog box for selecting files. The file can be a previously saved SPSS output or syntax file or a file created in another application and saved in text format. The file appears in a new syntax window.

Using SPSS Command Syntax in a Syntax Window

You can use any text editor or word processing software that saves files in text format to create a file of SPSS command syntax and then open the file in a syntax window. You can also use the dialog box interface to generate the basic command syntax and then edit the commands in the syntax window.

Pasting Command Syntax from Dialog Boxes

Use the Paste pushbutton to paste your dialog box selections into a syntax window. If you don't have an open syntax window, one opens automatically the first time you paste from a dialog box.

Pasting Variable Names from the Variables Dialog Box

You can use the Variables dialog box to copy variable names and then paste them into command syntax. For more information, see Chapter 10.

Running SPSS Commands

You can run single commands or groups of commands in the syntax window.

1. Select the commands you want to run. Using the mouse, use the click-and-drag method to highlight the commands. The highlighted area can begin anywhere in the first command and end anywhere in the last command, as shown in Figure 4.1.

   If you want to run only a single command, you can position the cursor anywhere in the command line. If you want to run all of the commands in the syntax window, you can choose Select All from the Edit menu.

2. Click on the Run Syntax tool on the toolbar.

Figure 4.1   Running selected commands

```
██▐    ▄▄▄▄▄▄▄▄▄▄ !untitled syntax ▄▄▄▄▄▄▄▄▄▄    ▐██
CROSSTABS                                              ⇧
  /TABLES=jobcat  BY sexrace
  /FORMAT= AVALUE NOINDEX BOX LABELS TABLES
  /CELLS= COUNT .
FREQUENCIES
  VARIABLES=jobcat sexrace edlevel .
MEANS
  TABLES=salbeg  BY sexrace  BY jobcat
  /CELLS MEAN STDDEV COUNT
  /FORMAT= LABELS .
DESCRIPTIVES
  VARIABLES=salbeg salnow
  /FORMAT=LABELS NOINDEX
  /STATISTICS=MEAN STDDEV MIN MAX
  /SORT=MEAN (A) .
                                                       ⇩
◁▐                                                   ▷▐
```

Highlight includes part of
two commands.
Both commands are run.

Multiple Syntax Windows

You can have multiple syntax windows, but there is only one **designated syntax window**. If you have more than one syntax window open, the Paste pushbutton pastes command syntax into the designated syntax window. By default, the first syntax window opened is the designated syntax window. To designate a different syntax window, make the syntax window the active window and click on the Designate Window tool on the toolbar or choose Designate Window from the Utilities menu.

All new commands that you paste are appended to the bottom of the text file in the designated syntax window. The window remains the designated syntax window until you select another. If there is no designated syntax window, a new one is automatically opened the next time you click on the Paste pushbutton.

Editing Output and Syntax Files

You can edit text in syntax and output windows using text-editing features similar to those used in word processing software. You can:

- Cut, copy, and paste blocks of text within and between text files and windows.
- Copy text to and from the Data Editor and other software applications.
- Search for and replace text strings.
- Change type fonts.

Selecting Text

There are several ways to select text in an output or syntax window:

- Click the mouse button and drag the mouse to select entire lines of text.
- Move the insertion point and then shift-click the mouse button.
- Option-click the mouse button and drag the mouse to select rectangular areas.
- Double-click in the left margin of an output block to select the entire output block for that command.
- Triple-click anywhere in a command in a syntax window to select the entire command.

Edit Menu

The following text-editing options are available with the Edit menu:

Undo. Undoes the previous action.

Cut. Cuts the highlighted text and puts it on the clipboard.

Copy. Copies the highlighted text onto the clipboard.

Copy Table. Copies the highlighted columns onto the clipboard in tab-delimited format. This is useful for copying output tables (for example, frequency distributions, means tables, etc.) into spreadsheet or word processing files.

Paste. Pastes the contents of the clipboard into the file at the insertion point. **Paste** is enabled only if there is something on the clipboard that can be pasted into the active window.

Clear. Cuts the highlighted text without putting it on the clipboard. (You cannot paste the text anywhere else.)

Select All. Select the entire contents of the active output or syntax window.

Search for Text. Searches for a text string in the active syntax or output window. This opens the Search dialog box.

Replace Text. Searches for and replaces a text string with a new text string. This opens the Replace dialog box.

Round. Rounds any numbers in the highlighted area. This opens the Round dialog box.

Add Page Break. Adds a page break at the current cursor location in the active output window.

Add Output Break. Adds an output break at the current cursor location in the active output window.

Search for Text

To search for a text string in a syntax or output window, from the menus choose:

Edit
  Search for Text...

This opens the Search for Text dialog box, as shown in Figure 4.2.

Figure 4.2   Search for Text dialog box

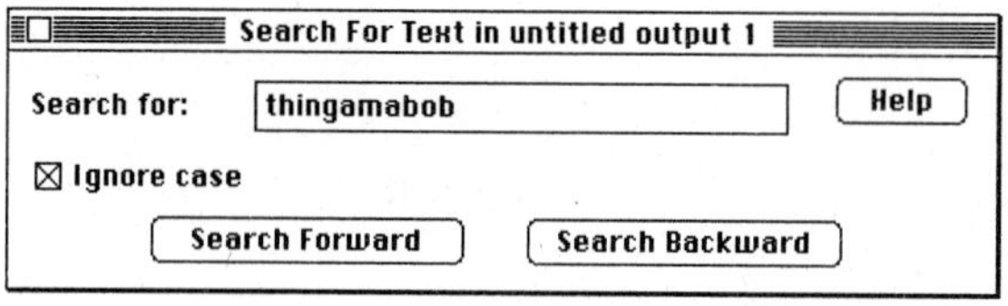

Search Forward. Searches forward from the cursor location to the end of the file.

Search Backward. Searches backward from the cursor location to the beginning of the file.

The following option is also available:

❏ **Ignore case**. By default, SPSS searches for any occurrence of the specified text string, regardless of case. If you want to restrict the search to occurrences that match the case as entered, deselect this default setting.

Replace Text

To search for a text string and replace it with another text string, from the menus choose:

Edit
  Replace Text...

This opens the Replace Text dialog box, as shown in Figure 4.3.

Figure 4.3   Replace Text dialog box

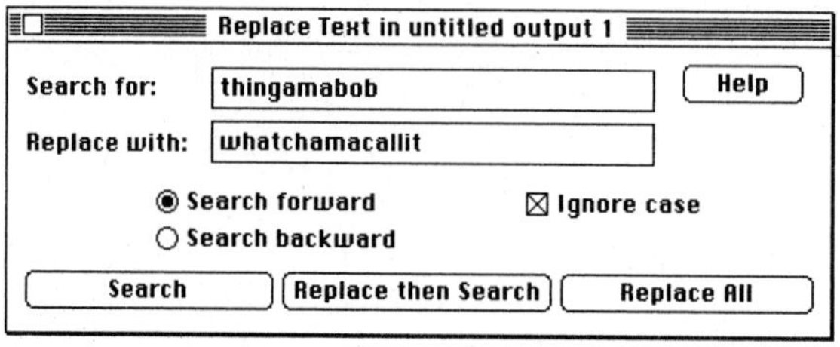

Search. Finds the next occurrence of the text string.

Replace then Search. Replaces the current occurrence of the text string and searches for the next one. If an occurrence of the text string is not currently highlighted in the syntax or output window, click on Search to find and highlight the text string.

Replace All. Replaces all occurrences of the text string from the cursor location to the end (or beginning) of the file.

For search direction, you can choose one of the following alternatives:

○ **Search forward**. Searches forward from the cursor location to the end of the file.

○ **Search backward**. Searches backward from the cursor location to the beginning of the file.

The following option is also available:

❏ **Ignore case**. By default, SPSS searches for any occurrence of the specified text string, regardless of case. If you want to restrict the search to occurrences that match the case as entered, deselect this default setting.

Round

To round or truncate highlighted values in a syntax or output window, from the menus choose:

Edit
  Round...

This opens the Round dialog box, as shown in Figure 4.4.

Figure 4.4   Round dialog box

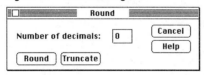

Number of decimals. Enter an integer value from 0 to 9. The default value is 0.

Round. Rounds values in the highlighted area to the specified number of decimals.

Truncate. Truncates values in the highlighted area at the specified number of decimals.

Type Fonts

To change the font type, style, and size of text in a syntax or output window:

1. Make the syntax or output window the active window.

2. From the menus choose:

Utilities
  Fonts...

This opens the Fonts dialog box, which contains a list of the available fixed-pitch fonts. Font changes are applied to all of the text in the active window. Fonts cannot be selectively applied to portions of the file. (See Chapter 10 for more information on fonts.)

Copying and Pasting Output into Other Applications

You can copy and paste SPSS output into other applications, such as a word processing program, in several ways:

- Highlight the text you want, select Copy from the Edit menu, paste it into the other application, and then apply a fixed-pitch font to the block of text for proper alignment. If the output contains box characters (such as the line-drawing characters in crosstabulations), these characters are converted to typewriter characters.

- Highlight a block of tabular output, such as a frequency table, select Copy Table from the Edit menu, paste the text into the other application, and then adjust the tab stops (if necessary). This is effective only for aligned columns of text. If the output contains any box characters, those characters are ignored.

- Select a fixed-pitch, TrueType font (for example, Monaco) for the output display, select Copy from the Edit menu, select Paste Special from the other application's Edit menu, and then select PICT or Picture from the Paste Special dialog box. All text is correctly aligned, and any box-drawing characters are preserved. However, since the text is treated as a picture, you cannot edit the contents.

Note: Paste Special may not be available for some applications. This feature enables the application to paste the contents of the clipboard as a "picture."

Saving Output and Syntax Files

New syntax and output files and changes to existing files are not saved unless you explicitly save them. To save changes to an existing output or syntax file:

1. Make the syntax or output window containing the file the active window.

2. From the menus choose:

File
  Save

The modified file is saved, overwriting the previous version of the file.

Save As New File

To save a new syntax or output file or to save changes to an existing file as a new file:

1. Make the syntax or output window containing the file the active window.

2. From the menus choose:

   File
     Save As...

This opens a standard dialog box for saving files. Type or select a name and directory for the file.

Saving Output in Text Format

By default, SPSS output is saved in SPSS Output format, which contains some special characters that can't be read by other applications, such as text editors. These special characters include:

- Box characters used to draw solid vertical and horizontal lines (such as a crosstabulation table)

- Output and page markers

To save output as plain text (output of type TEXT):

1. Make the syntax or output window containing the file the active window.

2. From the menus choose:

   File
     Save As...

3. In the dialog box for saving output, select TEXT from the pop-up list of file types.

Output and page markers are deleted from the saved text file, and box characters are converted to standard text characters.

5 Overview of the SPSS Chart Facility

High-resolution charts and plots are created by the procedures on the Graphs menu and by many of the procedures on the Statistics menu. This chapter provides an overview of the SPSS chart facility, including the following information:

- **Chart creation and modification.** An overview of creation and modification of a simple chart.
- **Chart Carousel.** Discussion of the SPSS window that holds and displays charts as they are created. You can view, save, copy, and print charts from this window.
- **Chart definition global options.** Definition options that apply to all or most charts, including titles and subtitles, footnotes, missing data values, case labels, and templates.
- **Rotated vertical text.** Font considerations for vertical text.

How to Create and Modify a Chart

Before you can create a chart, you need to get your data into SPSS. You can enter the data in the Data Editor, open a previously saved SPSS data file, or read a spreadsheet, tab-delimited, spreadsheet, dBASE, or database file. The SPSS Tutorial has online examples of creating and modifying a chart. For more information about getting your data into SPSS, see Chapter 2.

Creating the Chart

After you get your data into SPSS, you can create a chart by selecting a chart type from the Graphs menu. This opens a chart dialog box, such as the Bar Charts dialog box shown in Figure 5.1.

Figure 5.1   Chart dialog box

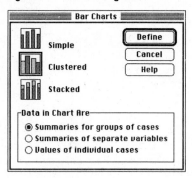

The dialog box contains icons for various types of charts and a list of data structures. Chart types and data structures are described in the *SPSS Base System User's Guide, Part 2* and in the Help system. Clicking on Define opens a chart definition dialog box, such as the one shown in Figure 5.2.

Figure 5.2   Chart definition dialog box

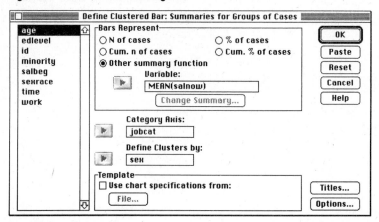

In this dialog box, you can select the variables appropriate for the chart and choose options you want. For information about the various choices, click on Help.

The chart appears in the Chart Carousel, as shown in Figure 5.3.

Figure 5.3   Chart in Chart Carousel

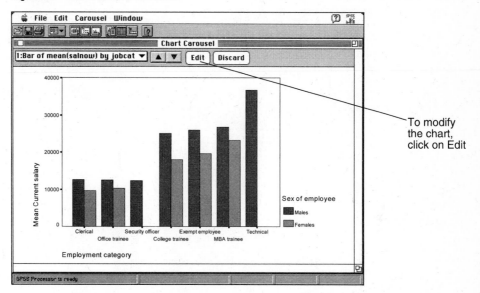

The Chart Carousel is a holding area for newly entered charts. The Chart Carousel menu bar replaces the main menu bar, and the core tools are displayed on the toolbar. You can save and print the chart directly from the Chart Carousel and use it in a report. You can also switch to a chart window to make modifications that will enhance the chart so that it will deliver a clearer message.

Modifying the Chart

The first step in chart modification is to transfer the chart from the Chart Carousel to a chart window. To do this, click on Edit. This places the chart in a chart window, as shown in Figure 5.4.

Figure 5.4   Original chart in chart window

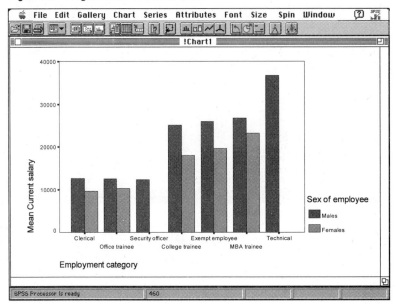

Notice that the Chart Editor menu bar replaces that of the Chart Carousel and the chart tools are on the toolbar.

You can modify any part of the chart or use the gallery to change to another type of chart illustrating the same data. Chart modification and the Chart Editor menus are described in detail in Chapter 6, Chapter 7, and Chapter 8. Some typical modifications include the following:

- Edit axis titles and labels.
- Edit the legend, which identifies the colors or patterns of the bars.
- Add a title.
- Change the location of the bar origin line.
- Add annotation.
- Add an outer frame.

These modifications were applied to the chart in Figure 5.4 and the results are shown in Figure 5.5.

Figure 5.5   Modified chart

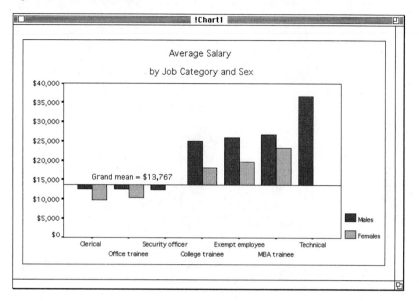

To print the chart or copy it into a document, see Chapter 9.

Chart Carousel

The previous sections described the process of creating a chart. The remaining sections of this chapter describe features that apply to all or most chart types. High-resolution charts and plots are initially displayed in the Chart Carousel, as shown in Figure 5.6. This is a holding area from which you can save the chart in various formats, discard it, print it, copy it to the clipboard, or transfer it to a chart window for editing.

Figure 5.6　Chart Carousel

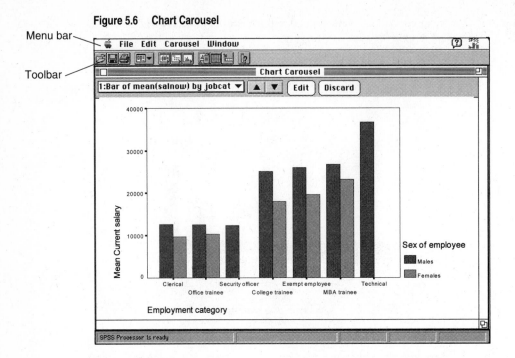

Chart Carousel Menus

When the Chart Carousel is the active window, its menu bar replaces the main menu bar. The Chart Carousel menu bar contains the following menus:

File. Use the File menu to create a new SPSS file, open an existing file, save one or more of the charts, or print the current chart or all charts.

Save As opens the Save As dialog box, which lets you select a name and a directory for the current chart. Charts are saved in SPSS chart format. You can also save all of the charts in the Carousel in one step, either when you close the Carousel or when you exit from SPSS. For more information, see "Saving Charts in the Chart Carousel" on p. 79.

Print opens a standard dialog box for printing. See Chapter 9 for more information.

Edit. Use the Edit menu to change your Graphics preferences (see Chapter 11) or to copy the chart to the clipboard.

Carousel. Use the Carousel menu to move the current chart to a chart window for editing or to move from chart to chart within the Carousel. You can redraw the current chart by selecting Refresh. You can also accomplish most of these tasks by clicking on tools in the Chart Carousel, as described in the section below.

Window. Use the Window menu to select various SPSS windows, just as on the main menu bar.

Chart Carousel Tools

Several tools appear within the Chart Carousel window. These tools duplicate functions that can be accessed from the Carousel menu. The tools behave as follows:

⬇ **Select.** Opens a drop-down list, from which you can choose one of the charts. The selected chart becomes the current chart.

▼ **Next.** Selects the next chart in the Carousel as the current chart.

▲ **Previous.** Selects the previous chart in the Carousel as the current chart.

Edit. Removes the current chart from the Carousel and places it in its own chart window for editing. From the chart window, you can modify most chart attributes, including colors, fonts, orientation, and type of chart displayed (see Chapter 6, Chapter 7, and Chapter 8).

Discard. Removes the current chart from the Carousel and discards it.

Saving Charts in the Chart Carousel

From the Chart Carousel, you can save only the current chart or save several charts.

Saving the current chart. To save only the current chart in the Chart Carousel, from the menus choose:

File
  Save As...

This opens a standard dialog box for saving files.

Saving several charts. To save one or more of the charts and also close the Chart Carousel, from the menus choose:

File
  Close

This opens a standard dialog box for saving files. You can access this dialog box either when you close the Carousel or when you exit from SPSS.

   To save one chart at a time, type or select a filename and directory for the current chart. After the current chart is saved, the name of the next chart is displayed near the bottom of the dialog box. You can either save or discard each chart in turn. You can cycle through the charts without saving each one by clicking on Next Chart. This deletes each chart in turn.

If you want to save all of the charts, click on Save All. This opens the Save All Root Name dialog box, as shown in Figure 5.7.

Figure 5.7   Save All Root Name dialog box

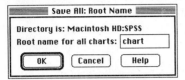

Type a root name of one to five characters. SPSS will append a unique number for each chart. For example, suppose you are working with food data and you type *food* as the root name. The filenames for the charts will be *food1*, *food2*, etc. After the charts are saved, you can edit them by opening each one from the File menu.

Chart Definition Global Options

When you are defining a chart, the specific chart definition dialog box usually contains the pushbuttons Titles and Options, and a Template group, as shown in Figure 5.8. These global options are available for most charts, regardless of type. They are not available for normal P-P plots, normal Q-Q plots, sequence charts, or time series charts.

Figure 5.8   A chart definition dialog box

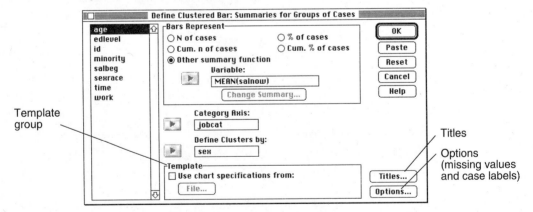

The Titles dialog box allows you to specify titles, subtitles, and footnotes. Clicking on Options allows you to control the treatment of missing values for most charts and case labels for scatterplots. You can apply a template of previously selected attributes either when you are defining the chart or after the chart has been created. The next few sections describe how to define these characteristics at the time you define the chart.

Titles, Subtitles, and Footnotes

In any chart, you can define two title lines, one subtitle line, and two footnote lines as part of your original chart definition. To specify titles or footnotes while defining a chart, click on Titles in the chart definition dialog box, as shown in Figure 5.8. This opens the Titles dialog box, as shown in Figure 5.9.

Figure 5.9   Titles dialog box

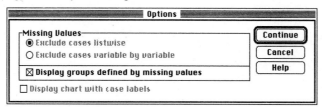

Each line can be up to 72 characters long. The number of characters that will actually fit in the chart depends upon the font and size. Most titles are left justified by default and, if too long, are cropped on the right. Pie chart titles, by default, are center justified and, if too long, are cropped at both ends.

You can also add, delete, or revise text lines, as well as change their font, size, and justification, within the Chart Editor (see Chapter 6).

Options

The Options dialog box provides options for treatment of missing values and display of case labels, as shown in Figure 5.10. This dialog box is available from the chart definition dialog box (see Figure 5.8).

Figure 5.10   Options dialog box

The availability of each option depends on your previous choices. Missing-value options are not available for charts using values of individual cases or for histograms. The case-labels display option is available only for a scatterplot that has a variable selected for case labels.

Missing Values. If you selected summaries of separate variables for a categorical chart or if you are creating a scatterplot, you can choose one of the following alternatives for exclusion of cases having missing values:

○ **Exclude cases listwise.** If any of the variables in the chart has a missing value for a given case, the whole case is excluded from the chart.

○ **Exclude cases variable by variable.** If a selected variable has any missing values, the cases having those missing values are excluded when the variable is analyzed.

The following option is also available for missing values:

❏ **Display groups defined by missing values.** If there are missing values in the data for variables used to define categories or subgroups, user-missing values (values identified as missing by the user) and system-missing values are included together in a category labeled *Missing*. The "missing" category is displayed on the category axis or in the legend, adding, for example, an extra bar, a slice to a pie chart, or an extra box to a boxplot. In a scatterplot, missing values add a "missing" category to the set of markers. If there are no missing values, the "missing" category is not displayed.

This option is selected by default. If you want to suppress display after the chart is drawn, select Displayed from the Series menu and move the categories you want suppressed to the Omit group. (See sections "Bar, Line, and Area Chart Displayed Data" on p. 98 through "Histogram Displayed Data" on p. 108 in Chapter 6.)

This option is not available for an overlay scatterplot or for single-series charts in which the data are summarized by separate variables.

To see the difference between listwise and variable-by-variable exclusion of missing values, consider Figure 5.11, which shows a bar chart for each of the two options. The charts were created from a version of the employee data file that was edited to have some system-missing (blank) values in the variables for current salary and job category. In some other cases of the job category variable, the value 9 was entered and defined as missing. For both charts, the option Display groups defined by missing values is selected, which adds the category *Missing* to the other job categories displayed. In each chart, the values of the summary function, *Number of cases*, are displayed in the bar labels.

Figure 5.11 Examples of missing-data treatment in charts

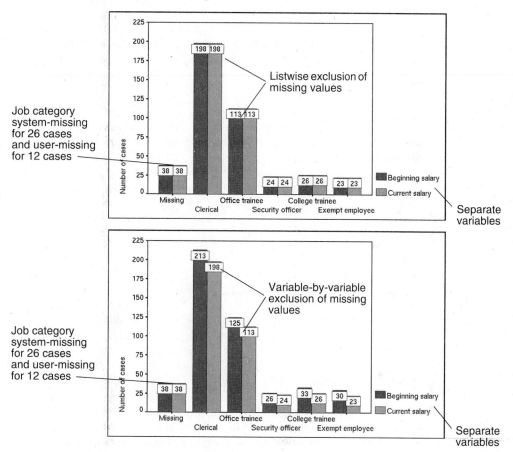

In both charts, 26 cases have a system-missing value for the job category and 12 cases have the user-missing value (9). In the listwise chart, the number of cases is the same for both variables in each bar cluster because whenever a value was missing, the case was excluded for all variables. In the variable-by-variable chart, the number of nonmissing cases for each variable in a category is plotted without regard to missing values in other variables.

The final selection in the Options dialog box controls the status of case labels when a scatterplot is first displayed.

❏ **Display chart with case labels.** When this option is selected, all case labels are displayed when a scatterplot is created. By default, it is deselected—that is, the default scatterplot is displayed without labels. If you select this option, case labels may overlap.

Chart Templates

You can apply many of the attributes and text elements from one chart to another. This allows you to modify one chart, save that chart, and then use it as a template to create a number of other similar charts.

To use a template when creating a chart, select Use chart specifications from (in the Template group in the chart definition dialog box shown in Figure 5.8), and click on File. This opens a standard file selection dialog box.

To apply a template to a chart already in a chart window, from the menus choose:

File
  Apply Chart Template...

This opens a standard file selection dialog box. Select a file to use as a template. If you are creating a new chart, the filename you select is displayed in the Template group when you return to the chart definition dialog box.

A template is used to borrow the format from one chart and apply it to the new chart you are generating. In general, any formatting information from the old chart that can apply to the new chart will automatically apply. For example, if the old chart is a clustered bar chart with bar colors modified to yellow and green and the new chart is a multiple line chart, the lines will be yellow and green. If the old chart is a simple bar chart with drop shadows and the new chart is a simple line chart, the lines will not have drop shadows because drop shadows don't apply to line charts. If there are titles in the template chart but not in the new chart, you will get the titles from the template chart. If there are titles defined in the new chart, they will override the titles in the template chart.

❏ **Apply title and footnote text.** Applies the text of the title and footnotes of the template to the current chart, overriding any text defined in the Titles dialog box in the current chart. The attributes of the title and footnotes (font, size, and color) are applied whether or not this item is selected. This check box appears only if you are applying the template in a chart window, not when creating a new chart.

Rotated Vertical Chart Text

Axis, category, and scale labels displayed in vertical format are rotated for TrueType fonts (indicated by outline font in the Size menu) and stacked for bitmap fonts. To switch from stacked to rotated text (or vice versa), you must change the type of font used. Figure 5.12 shows both rotated TrueType and stacked bitmap fonts displayed in a chart.

Figure 5.12   Fonts in labels

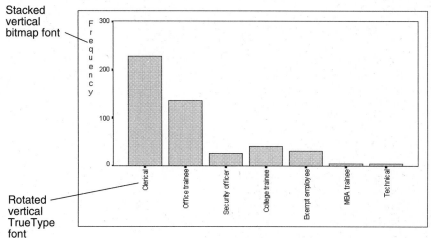

6 Modifying Charts

After creating a chart and viewing it in the Chart Carousel, you may wish to modify it, either to obtain more information about the data or to enhance the chart for presentation. The chart modification capabilities of SPSS allow you to select data, change chart types, add information, and alter chart appearance to accomplish both of those goals.

Two brief examples are given in this chapter. The first example illustrates a process for exploring data relationships graphically; the second, enhancing a bar chart for presentation. Following the two examples in this chapter are detailed explanations of the following:

- Changing chart types (Gallery menu)
- Selecting and arranging data (Series menu)
- Case identification in scatterplots and boxplots
- Spin mode in 3-D scatterplots

Chapter 7 discusses facilities for modifying chart elements by using the Chart menu. Chapter 8 discusses changing the attributes of chart elements and text by using the Attributes, Font, and Size menus.

Exploring Data with the Chart Editor

Figure 6.1 shows a preliminary scatterplot matrix of graduation rate, verbal SAT score, and student–faculty ratio in 250 colleges and universities.

Figure 6.1   Scatterplot matrix of gradrate, verbal, and facratio

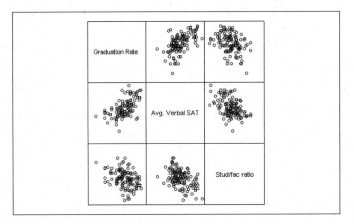

Two of the available options for scatterplots, adding axis labels and linear regression lines, help to make relationships more apparent, as illustrated in Figure 6.2.

Figure 6.2   Scatterplot matrix with labels and regression lines

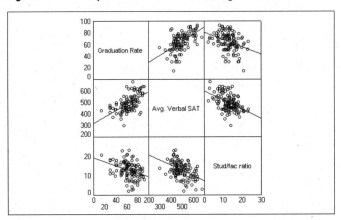

For a closer look at the relationship between schools' graduation rates and the average SAT verbal test scores of their students, we can turn to the Gallery menu and select a bivariate (simple) scatterplot of those variables. In the bivariate scatterplot, we can see more detail (see Figure 6.3).

Figure 6.3   Scatterplot of gradrate and verbal

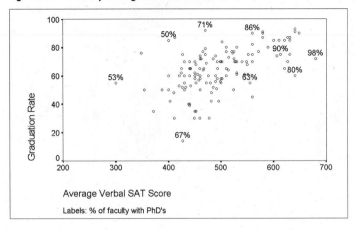

Individual case labels have been turned on with the Point Selection tool. We might want to look more closely at the univariate distribution of the two variables, which we can do by returning to the Gallery menu and selecting a histogram (see Figure 6.4).

Figure 6.4   Histograms of verbal and gradrate

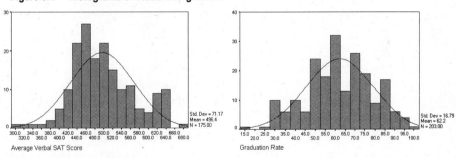

Enhancing Charts for Presentation

Although charts as originally generated by SPSS contain the requested information in a logical format, they may require some changes to make the presentation clearer or more dramatic. Figure 6.5 is the unedited clustered bar chart of *verbal* and *math* (the average verbal and math SAT scores for each university) by *comp* (level of competitiveness).

Figure 6.5   Default bar chart of verbal and math by comp

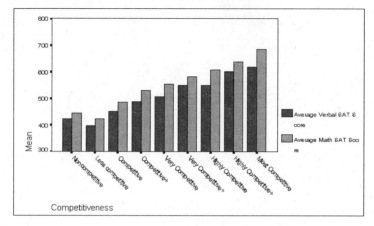

While the information is clear, at least some changes are desirable to prepare the chart for presentation. The following modifications create the chart shown in Figure 6.6:

- A title is added.
- 3-D effect is selected for the bars.
- Both axis titles are removed, since the information they contain appears elsewhere in the chart. This allows more room for the chart itself and the chart enlarges itself automatically.
- The noncompetitive category is removed.
- Several labels are removed from the category axis and the orientation of the remaining labels is changed. This makes the labels easier to read, yet still conveys the essential information.
- The legend labels are edited to remove unnecessary information.
- The range of the scale axis is enlarged to start at 200, the lowest possible SAT score, in order to give a better representation of the relative differences between schools in each competitiveness level.
- Reference lines and annotations are added to indicate the overall averages for the two SAT tests. (These averages are easily obtained by leaving the chart window for a moment to run descriptive statistics from the Statistics menu.)

Figure 6.6   Enhanced bar chart

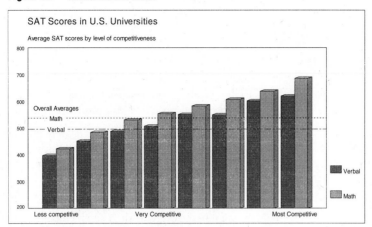

Editing in a Chart Window

All modifications to charts are done in a chart window. You open a chart window by selecting Edit from the Chart Carousel or by opening a previously saved chart from the File menu. Closing a chart window closes the chart.

Several chart windows can be open at the same time, each containing a single chart. The exact number depends on your system and on how many other windows are open at the time. If you see a message telling you that there are not enough system resources, you can close some windows to free resources.

Chart Menus

When a chart window is active, the Chart Editor menu bar replaces the main menu bar.

The Chart Editor menu bar contains nine menus:

File. From the File menu, you can save or export the chart, print it, or apply specifications from an existing chart template.

Edit. From the Edit menu, you can copy the chart to the clipboard.

You can also choose Preferences to open the Preferences dialog box (see Chapter 11). Graphics preferences include global chart characteristics such as preferred type font, use of color versus pattern in lines and areas, and use of grid lines. If you select an aspect ratio, it applies immediately to all charts currently in chart windows or in the Chart Carousel. The other preferences are applied as each chart is initially drawn; they also apply to all charts currently in the Chart Carousel. They do not apply to a chart that is already in a chart window for editing or to saved charts.

The Edit menu does not include items for modifying charts; the following menus contain those items.

Gallery. From the Gallery menu, you can select another compatible chart type to display the data in your chart. After selecting a new chart type, you can click on Replace to replace the current chart or click on New to create another chart in a new window. See "Changing Chart Types (Gallery Menu)" on p. 94 for more information.

Chart. From the Chart menu, you can modify many of the layout and labeling characteristics of your chart, such as the scaling and labeling of axes, all titles and labels, and inner and outer frames. You can also swap axes of plots, explode one or more slices of a pie chart, and edit colors. See Chapter 7 for more information.

Series. From the Series menu, you can select data series and categories to display or omit. Only data elements present in the original chart can be included. For bar, line, and area charts, you can select whether each series should be displayed as a line, an area, or a set of bars. For line charts, you can change the treatment of missing values and select styles of interpolation. See "Selecting and Arranging Data (Series Menu)" on p. 97 for more information.

Attributes. From the Attributes menu, you can open a set of palettes from which you can select fill patterns, colors, marker type and size, and line style and width. To use these, you click on the element whose attributes you want to change. Then you can make a selection from any appropriate palette. See Chapter 8 for more information.

Font. From the Font menu, you can change the font of text elements in the chart. See Chapter 8 for more information.

Size. From the Size menu, you can change the font size of text elements in the chart. See Chapter 8 for more information.

Spin. From the Spin menu, you can rotate 3-D charts. See "Spin for 3-D Scatterplots" on p. 118 for more information.

Selecting Objects to Modify

The objects that make up a chart fall into two general categories:

- **Series objects** are the bars, lines, and markers that represent the data. They are always selected and manipulated as a series.
- **Chart objects** are the layout and labeling components of the chart—everything other than the series objects.

To modify one of these objects, double-click on it in the chart. If you double-click on a series object, the Displayed Data dialog box for the current chart type is opened (see "Selecting and Arranging Data (Series Menu)" on p. 97). If you double-click on a chart object, one of the dialog boxes from the Chart menu is opened: Axis if you have selected an axis, Title if you have selected a title, and so on (see "Selecting and Arranging Data (Series Menu)" on p. 97). If you double-click on an object for which a specific dialog box does not exist, or if you double-click away from any object, the Options dialog box for the current chart type is opened.

Instead of double-clicking on objects, you can open the series dialog boxes from the Series and Chart menus. A few items on those menus can be accessed only from the menus, not by double-clicking on an object or clicking on a tool.

The following items are available only from the Chart menu:

- Bar Spacing
- Title, Footnote, and Annotation (when none appear in the chart)
- Toggles for the Inner Frame and Outer Frame
- Edit available colors

The following item is available only from the Series menu:

- Transpose Data

Both series and chart objects have **attributes** such as color and pattern. To modify the attributes of an object, select the object with a single mouse click. There is no keyboard mechanism for selecting objects. If the object is within the chart itself, **handles** (small, solid-black rectangles) indicate which object is selected. For objects outside the chart axes, such as titles or labels, a **selection rectangle** indicates that an object is selected. Selection of an inner or outer frame is indicated by handles.

Applying Attributes

After an object is selected, select a palette from the Attributes menu. Figure 6.7 shows handles and the Attributes menu. You can apply attributes from as many palettes as you choose; the object stays selected until you select another or click somewhere away from any object. See Chapter 8 for more details.

Figure 6.7   Bar chart showing selection handles and colors palette

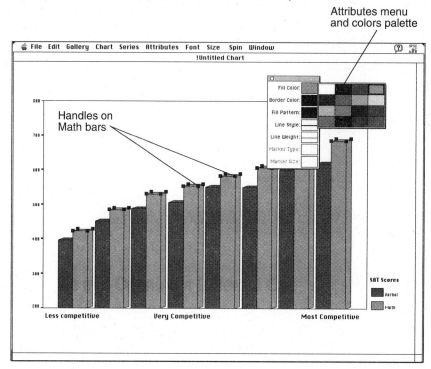

Changing Chart Types (Gallery Menu)

The Gallery menu allows you to change from one chart type to another. The choices are primarily the same as those available from the Graph menu, with a few additions. (See the *SPSS Base System User's Guide, Part 2* for detailed descriptions of chart types.)

Additional Chart Types

Some types of charts are available only after you have created a chart. These include mixed charts and exploded pie charts.

Mixed Charts. Mixed charts are available on the Gallery menu. You can have bars, lines, and areas, all in the same chart, after defining a bar, line, or area multiple series chart. Figure 6.8 is an example of a mixed chart with both bars and lines.

Figure 6.8   Mixed chart

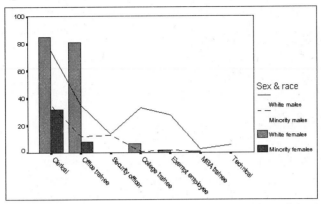

You can also define a mixed chart by choosing:

Series
  Displayed...

from the menus. For more information on mixed charts, see "Selecting and Arranging Data (Series Menu)" on p. 97.

Exploded Pie Chart. Exploded pie charts can be generated from the Pie Charts dialog box. To explode all slices of a pie chart at once, from the menus choose:

Gallery
  Pie...

This opens the Pie Charts dialog box. Click on **Exploded** and then click on **Replace** or **New**. Each slice of the pie is moved outward from the center, along a radius, as shown in Figure 6.9.

Figure 6.9   Exploded pie chart

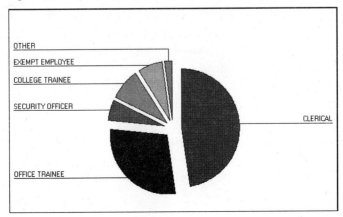

Changing Types

You can change freely among chart types, with the following restrictions:

- You must have enough data to draw the selected chart. Thus, you cannot change from a simple bar chart to a clustered bar chart if you have only one data series defined. However, if your original chart had more than one series, and you omitted all but one of those series to obtain the simple bar, you can change to a chart that requires multiple series. See "Selecting and Arranging Data (Series Menu)" on p. 97 for information on selecting series.

- You cannot change in either direction between categorical charts (bar, line, area, pie, and high-low charts) and plots based on casewise data (scatterplots and histograms).

- You cannot change from or into a boxplot. Thus, boxplot is not on the Gallery menu.

- You cannot change into an error bar chart, but you can change from an error bar chart into another categorical chart if there are enough data series for the type of chart selected.

If there is an obvious transition between the display of series in the current chart and the display of series in the selected chart, the new chart is drawn automatically. If not, the Displayed Data dialog box for the new chart opens for you to indicate how to display the series. For example:

- Changing from a single series chart such as a simple bar, simple line, or pie to another single series chart is automatic.

- Changing from a clustered bar chart to a simple bar chart opens the Displayed Data dialog box for you to indicate which series to plot.

- Changing from a clustered or stacked bar chart to a multiple line chart is automatic. All series in the bar chart are plotted as lines.

- Changing from a simple bar chart to a multiple line chart opens the Displayed Data dialog box if you have series from your original chart not displayed in the simple bar chart. See "Selecting and Arranging Data (Series Menu)" on p. 97 for more information about omitting and restoring series.

- Changing from a clustered bar chart to a clustered range bar chart opens the Displayed Data dialog box for you to select which series are to be paired.

- Changing from a range bar chart to a difference line chart opens the Displayed Data dialog box for you to select which two series are to be displayed.

- Changing from a 3-D scatterplot to a scatterplot matrix is automatic. Changing from a scatterplot matrix to a simple scatterplot opens the Displayed Data dialog box.

- Changing into a mixed chart type always opens the Bar/Line/Area Displayed Data dialog box for you to indicate which series are to be displayed as bars, areas, or lines.

- Changing into a high-low chart always opens the Displayed Data dialog box.

You can change among bar, line, and area charts and create mixed charts within the Bar/Line/Area Displayed Data dialog box without using the Gallery menu (see "Bar,

Line, and Area Chart Displayed Data" on p. 98). You can create simple bar, line, or area charts from multiple versions of the charts by omitting all but one series. You can also change between stacked bars and clustered bars in the Bar/Line/Areas Options dialog box (see "Bar/Line/Area Options" on p. 122 in Chapter 7). To change to a pie chart, however, you must use the Gallery menu.

You cannot change among scatterplot types by adding or deleting series; you must use the Gallery menu. For example, if you omit all but two series in a matrix scatterplot, you are left with a 2×2 matrix. To make a simple scatterplot from the same data, from the menus choose:

Gallery
  Scatter...
    Simple

Each type of scatterplot has its own Displayed Data dialog box.

See "Bar, Line, and Area Chart Displayed Data" on p. 98 through "Histogram Displayed Data" on p. 108 for more information about displayed data.

Inheritance of Attributes and Other Chart Elements

When you change from one chart type to another, if an attribute in the current chart is applicable to the new chart, it is preserved. For example, if you change from clustered bars to multiple lines, the series represented by red bars is now represented by a red line and the green bars translate to a green line.

If a change in displayed data or in chart type makes a current chart specification invalid, that specification is set to the default. For example, suppose you are changing a clustered bar chart to a stacked bar chart. The range and increment on the scale axis are no longer valid and the stacked bar defaults are used.

Selecting and Arranging Data (Series Menu)

The Series menu allows you to modify your chart by selecting data and reassigning data elements within the chart. All of the data must exist within the original chart; you cannot add new data in the Chart Editor. You also cannot change values within the data. The options available vary by chart type:

- For bar, line, and area charts, you can omit data series and categories as long as enough data remain to generate the chart, and change the order of series and categories. You can specify for each series individually whether it is to be displayed as a bar, line, or area chart. You can also transpose the data so that series become categories and categories become series.

- For a line chart, you can select an interpolation style and display or hide markers. You can also decide whether the line should be broken or connected at a point where there is missing data.

- For pie charts, you can omit categories (slices). If the original chart defined more than one data series, you can select the series to be displayed.

- For boxplots, series operations are not available.

- For scatterplots, you can reassign series to axes, omitting those not needed in the plot. You cannot omit individual values within a series. Since the assignment of series to axes differs for each type of scatterplot, there are different Displayed Data dialog boxes for each type of scatterplot.

- For histograms, if the original chart was a scatterplot with more than one series, you can select which one of the series is to be displayed.

All of these options, except transposing data, are specified in Displayed Data dialog boxes, which are specific to the chart type and are discussed in the following sections.

When you choose:

Series
  Transpose

data transposition takes place without further query.

Cumulative Distributions in Charts

Data distributions are never recalculated in the Chart Editor. Thus, removing categories from a cumulative distribution, for example, will not change the values of the remaining categories. Cumulative distributions in pie charts, or in the scale dimension of stacked bar and area charts, will yield charts whose interpretation is unclear.

Bar, Line, and Area Chart Displayed Data

To arrange the data in a bar, line, area, or mixed chart, from the menus choose:

Series
  Displayed...

This opens a Displayed Data dialog box. Figure 6.10 shows the Displayed Data dialog box for the bar chart in Figure 6.6.

Figure 6.10   Bar/Line/Area Displayed Data dialog box

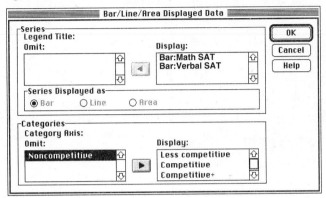

The controls in the Bar/Line/Area Displayed Data dialog box fall into two groups: those having to do with series and those having to do with categories.

Series. The legend title, if any, is listed for your information. (To change it, see "Legends" on p. 154 in Chapter 7.) Since multiple series are identified in the legend, this title may help to clarify what the series represent. The series are displayed in two list boxes: those omitted from the chart and those displayed in the chart. To move a series from one list box to the other, select it and click on ▶ or ◀. You must have at least one series displayed for the OK pushbutton to be enabled.

The order of series on the Display list controls the order of bars within clusters, the order of segments within stacked bars, the order of stacked areas, and the order of legend items for all bar, area, and line charts. You can reorder the Display list by moving categories to the Omit list and then moving them back again in the new order. In mixed charts, lines appear in the legend above areas and areas above bars.

Series Displayed as. On the list of series, each series name is followed by a colon and the word *Bar*, *Line*, or *Area* to indicate how it will be displayed when the chart is next drawn. To change the display for a series, select the series and then select one of the Series Displayed as alternatives. The chart in Figure 6.11 was derived from the chart in Figure 6.8 by changing the lines to areas and stacking the bars.

Categories. You can select categories to omit or display in the same way you select series. Displayed categories form the category axis in the order listed. You can reorder the Display list by moving categories to the Omit list and then moving them back in the new order.

Figure 6.11   Mixed chart with bars and areas

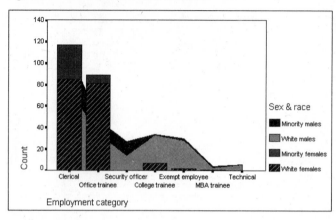

Pie Chart Displayed Data

To adjust the display of series and categories in a pie chart, from the menus choose:

Series
  Displayed...

This opens the Pie Displayed Data dialog box, as shown in Figure 6.12.

Figure 6.12   Pie Displayed Data dialog box

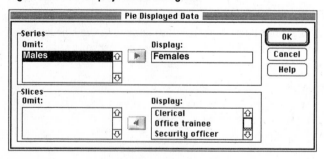

Series. If you created the chart as a pie chart, there is only one series listed. If you selected Pie from the Gallery menu with a multiple series chart, there are several series in the Omit group and one under Display. If you don't want the selected series, first move the series to the Omit group. Then select the series you want.

Slices. You can delete categories from the display by moving them to the Omit list in the Slices group. If you omit any categories, the size of each slice is recalculated, using only the categories to be displayed.

High-Low-Close Displayed Data

To adjust the display of data series in a high-low-close chart, from the menus choose:

Series
 Displayed...

This opens the High-Low-Close Displayed Data dialog box, as shown in Figure 6.13.

Figure 6.13   High-Low-Close Displayed Data dialog box

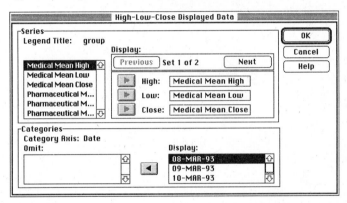

Series. The legend title, if any, is listed for your information. (To change it, see "Legends" on p. 154 in Chapter 7.) Since multiple series are identified in the legend, this title may help to clarify what the series represent. The series available are displayed in the list box on the left. The series displayed in the chart are grouped in sets of a pair of high and low series along with an optional close series. To move a series between a High, Low, or Close box and the list of available series, select it and click on ▶ or ◀. You must have at least one pair of high and low specifications for the OK pushbutton to be enabled. A close specification is optional.

To view additional high-low pairs or to specify a new set, click on Next or Previous. Duplicate sets of high-low-close specifications are not allowed. You can, however, use a series in more than one set, although you should be careful to select meaningful pairs.

Categories. The category axis title is listed for your information. You can select categories to omit or display. To move a category from one list box to the other, select it and click on ▶ or ◀. Displayed categories form the category axis in the order listed. You can reorder the Display list by moving categories to the Omit list and then moving them back in the new order.

Range Bar Displayed Data

To adjust the display of data series in a range bar chart, from the menus choose:

Series
  Displayed...

This opens the Range Bar Displayed Data dialog box, as shown in Figure 6.14.

Figure 6.14   Range Bar Displayed Data dialog box

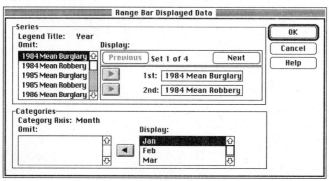

Series. The legend title, if any, is listed for your information. (To change the legend title, see "Legends" on p. 154 in Chapter 7.) Since multiple series are identified in the legend, this title may help to clarify what the series represent. The series available are displayed in the list box on the left. The series displayed in the chart are grouped in pairs of series. To copy a series between a pair box and the list of available series, select it and click on ▶ or ◀ . You must have at least one pair of specifications for the OK pushbutton to be enabled.

To view additional pairs or to specify a new pair, click on Next or Previous. Duplicate sets of pair specifications are not allowed. You can, however, use a series in more than one pair, although you should be careful to select meaningful pairs.

Categories. The category axis title is listed for your information. You can select categories to omit or display. To move a category from one list box to the other, select it and click on ▶ or ◀ . Displayed categories form the category axis in the order listed. You can reorder the Display list by moving categories to the Omit list and then moving them back in the new order.

Difference Line Displayed Data

To adjust the display of data series in a difference line chart, from the menus choose:

Series
  Displayed...

This opens the Difference Line Displayed Data dialog box, as shown in Figure 6.15.

Figure 6.15   Difference Line Displayed Data dialog box

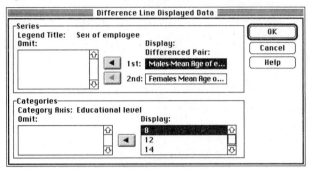

Series. The legend title, if any, is listed for your information. (To change it, see "Legends" on p. 154 in Chapter 7.) Since multiple series are identified in the legend, this title may help to clarify what the series represent. The series are displayed in two boxes: those omitted from the chart and those displayed in the chart. To move a series between the Omit list box and one of the Differenced Pair boxes, select it and click on ► or ◄. You must have two series displayed for the OK pushbutton to be enabled.

Categories. You can select categories to omit or display in the same way you select series. Displayed categories form the category axis in the order listed. You can reorder the Display list by moving categories to the Omit list and then moving them back in the new order.

Error Bar Displayed Data

To adjust the display of data series in an error bar chart, from the menus choose:

Series
  Displayed...

This opens the Error Bar Displayed Data dialog box, as shown in Figure 6.16.

Figure 6.16   Error Bar Displayed Data dialog box

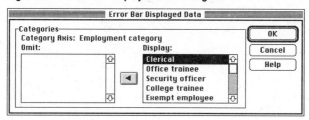

Categories. The category axis title is listed for your information. You can select categories to omit or display. To move a category from one list box to the other, select it and click on ▶ or ◀ . Displayed categories form the category axis in the order listed. You can reorder the Display list by moving categories to the Omit list and then moving them back in the new order.

Simple Scatterplot Displayed Data

To adjust the display of data series on a simple scatterplot, from the menus choose:

Series
  Displayed...

This opens the Simple Scatterplot Displayed Data dialog box, which controls the assignment of data series to the axes. You can use it to swap axes in a simple scatterplot. In changing to a simple scatterplot from a chart that includes more than two series, you can select the series you want to display on each axis. For example, suppose you have produced the overlay scatterplot shown in Figure 6.17, and you want to plot the verbal score against the math score.

Figure 6.17 Overlay scatterplot of SAT scores

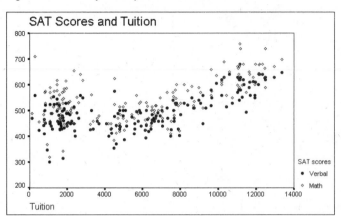

From the menus choose:

Gallery
  Scatter...

Then click on Simple and New. The Simple Scatterplot Displayed Data dialog box appears, as shown in Figure 6.18.

Figure 6.18 Simple Scatterplot Displayed Data dialog box

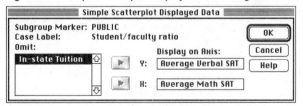

The variable that determines subgroup markers and the variable that supplies case labels (if either is assigned) are listed for your information. (Display of subgroup markers and case labels is controlled in Scatterplot Options. See "Overlay Scatterplot Options" on p. 134 in Chapter 7.)

To create a simple scatterplot where average verbal SAT is on the *x* axis and average math SAT is on the *y* axis, first select In-state Tuition under Display on Axis for X and click on ◄ to move it to the Omit list. Then select Average Verbal SAT and click on ► to move it to Display on Axis for Y. Both Y and X must be specified for the OK pushbutton to be enabled.

If the current chart data are limited to two variables, you can use this dialog box to swap the *x* and *y* axes by first moving the variables to the Omit list and then back to the appropriate Y and X boxes. When you have finished specifying variables, click on **OK** to display the new chart.

Overlay Scatterplot Displayed Data

To manipulate the display of series in an overlay scatterplot, from the menus choose:

Series
 Displayed...

This opens a dialog box similar to the one shown in Figure 6.19.

Figure 6.19   Overlay Scatterplot Displayed Data dialog box

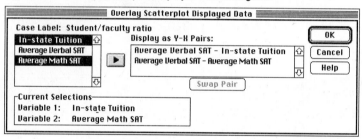

The case label variable, if any, is listed for your information. Underneath it is a box containing a list of the variables available for the chart. You cannot add any other variables. In the box labeled Display as Y-X Pairs are the pairs of variables plotted in the current chart. To remove a pair, select it and click on ◄ .

You can add pairs selected from the available variables. When you select one variable, it appears in the Current Selections group in the first position. The next variable you select appears in the second position. To deselect a variable, click on it again. When a pair of variables is in the Current Selections group and you click on ► , the pair appears in the Display box. For example, you might add the pair Average Math SAT-Average Verbal SAT. However, if you want the plots overlaid, you should consider the range on each axis. In the example just considered, the first two pairs listed have Tuition, which ranges into the thousands. SAT scores are in the hundreds, and the plot will look like a narrow line on the scale of thousands.

Clicking on **Swap Pair** reverses the axis assignments of a selected pair.

Scatterplot Matrix Displayed Data

If your chart is a scatterplot matrix, to change which series and categories are displayed, from the menus choose:

Series
 Displayed...

This opens a dialog box similar to the one shown in Figure 6.20.

Figure 6.20   Scatterplot Matrix Displayed Data dialog box

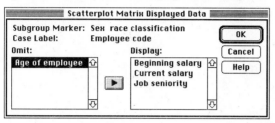

The subgroup marker and case label variable, if any, are listed for your information. The Display list box shows a list of available variables. To remove a variable from this list, select it and click on [◀] so that it moves to the Omit list. There must be at least two variables on the Display list for the OK button to be enabled.

You can reorder the Display list by moving categories to the Omit list and then moving them back in the new order.

3-D Scatterplot Displayed Data

To change the series displayed on a 3-D scatterplot, from the menus choose:

Series
 Displayed...

This opens the dialog box shown in Figure 6.21. This box is also displayed if you change to a 3-D scatterplot from the Gallery menu.

Figure 6.21   3-D Scatterplot Displayed Data dialog box

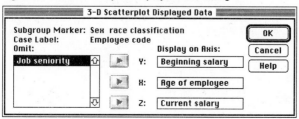

The subgroup marker and case label are listed for your information. The variable for each axis is listed under Display on Axis. To move a variable to the Omit list, select it and click on ◄ . You can swap the axes by moving the variables to the Omit list and then moving them back to the axes you want. In the default position, the y axis is vertical and perpendicular to the plane formed by the x and z axes.

Histogram Displayed Data

If a scatterplot is displayed (as in Figure 6.1), to obtain a histogram of one of the variables, from the menus choose:

Gallery
  Histogram...

This opens the Histogram Displayed Data dialog box, as shown in Figure 6.22. It can also be opened when a histogram is displayed by choosing:

Series
  Displayed...

Figure 6.22   Histogram Displayed Data dialog box

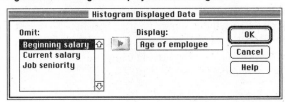

If you want to change the variable selected for display in the histogram, first select the variable in the Display box and move it to the Omit list. Then select another variable on the Omit list and move it to the Display box.

Transposing Data

In a multiple bar, line, or area chart, you can transpose series and categories. You can also transpose data in a high-low-close, range bar, or difference line chart. For example, in a clustered bar chart, the categories (designated on the category axis) become series (designated in the legend) and the series become categories. To do this, from the menus choose:

Series
  Transpose Data

The system redraws the chart if possible. If there is too much data or assignment is ambiguous, the appropriate Displayed Data dialog box is displayed.

An example is shown in Figure 6.23. The difference between transposing data and swapping axes is illustrated in "Swapping Axes in Two-Dimensional Charts" on p. 161 in Chapter 7. Data transposition is not available for boxplots, scatterplots, or histograms.

Figure 6.23   Example of transposing data

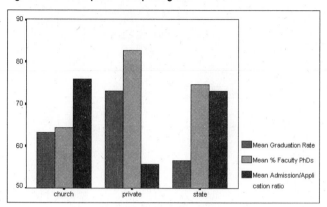

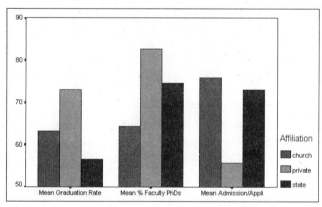

Line Interpolation

In a line chart, scatterplot, difference line chart, mean series in an error bar chart, or the close series in a high-low-close chart, several styles are available for connecting data points. To select a method used to connect the data points, click on the Interpolation tool, or from the menus choose:

Series
  Interpolation...

This opens the Line Interpolation dialog box, as shown in Figure 6.24. The Step, Jump, and Spline picture buttons each have a drop-down list. Examples of various types of interpolation are shown in Figure 6.25 on p. 111.

Figure 6.24   Line Interpolation dialog box

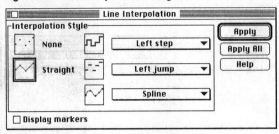

None. No lines connect the points.

Straight. The data points are connected in succession by straight lines. This is the default for line charts.

⬇ **Step.** Each data point has a horizontal line drawn through it, with vertical risers joining the steps. Selecting left, center, or right from the drop-down list specifies the location of the data point on the horizontal line.

⬇ **Jump**. Each data point has a horizontal line drawn through it, with no risers. Selecting left, center, or right from the drop-down list specifies the location of the data point on the horizontal line.

⬇ **Spline**. The data points are connected by a cubic spline. Lines are always drawn from left to right. For scatterplots, the parametric cubic form is used, and lines are drawn in order of data entry. On the Spline drop-down list are two more types of interpolation:

3rd-order Lagrange. Produces third-order Lagrange interpolations in which the third-order polynomial is fitted through the closest four points. The parametric cubic form is used with scatterplots.

5th-order Lagrange. Produces fifth-order Lagrange interpolations in which the fifth-order polynomial is fitted through the closest six points. The parametric form is used with scatterplots.

The following option is also available:

❏ **Display markers**. Displays markers at the data points. To change the style and size of the markers, see "Markers" on p. 171 in Chapter 8.

 For scatterplots, to obtain more interpolation types, click on the Options tool, or from the menus choose:

Chart
 Options...

Then select Total or Subgroups and click on Fit Options.

Figure 6.25   Examples of line interpolation with markers displayed

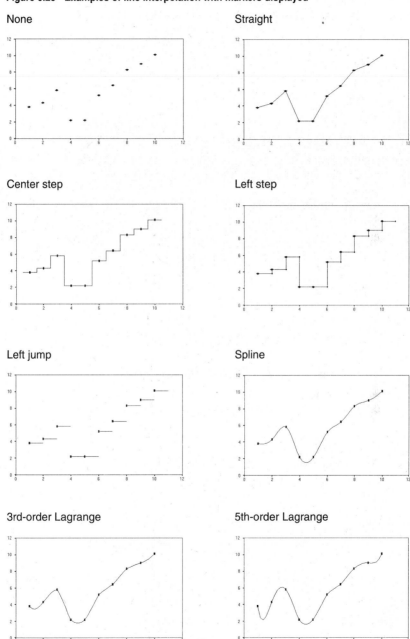

Handling Missing Data in a Line Chart

You can choose how to display a line chart that has some data missing. By default, the line has a break where the missing values should be. This is indicated by a check mark to the left of Break Lines at Missing on the Series menu. To connect all existing points, even though data are missing in between, from the menus choose:

Series
  Break Lines at Missing

The tool then changes to show a connected line. To break a line connected at missing values, click on the tool again.

In Figure 6.26, the top chart has no missing data. The other two charts each have a missing temperature value for Day 3. When Break Lines at Missing is selected, the missing data point is not connected within the chart line. This is the default for a line chart. When Break Lines at Missing is deselected, the surrounding points are connected, and it is easy to overlook the fact that there is no value there.

Figure 6.26 Missing data in a line chart

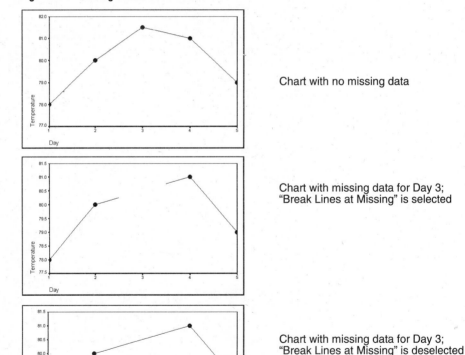

Chart with no missing data

Chart with missing data for Day 3;
"Break Lines at Missing" is selected

Chart with missing data for Day 3;
"Break Lines at Missing" is deselected

Case Identification in Scatterplots and Boxplots

While editing a scatterplot or boxplot, you can display all case labels or selected case labels for any of the points. You can also go directly from a point to its associated case in the Data Editor.

Point Selection

While editing a scatterplot or boxplot, you can change to **point selection mode** and click on a point to see its label (or case number). In this mode, when the original working data file that created the chart is still active, clicking on a point also selects the corresponding case in the Data Editor. In a boxplot, point selection applies only to outliers and extremes.

 This feature is available only when a scatterplot or boxplot is in a chart window (not in the Chart Carousel). To change to point selection mode, click on the Point Selection tool on the toolbar, as shown in Figure 6.27.

Figure 6.27   Point selection in a scatterplot

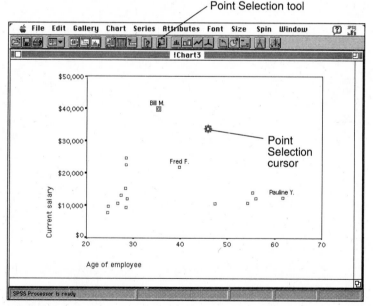

The cursor changes shape to show that the system is in point selection mode. The Point Selection tool is a toggle that turns the mode on or off.

In point selection mode, if you click on a point in the chart, the point is selected (highlighted) and a label is displayed. To turn off the label of a point, click on it again. If you click in an area away from all points, the selected point is deselected.

Multiple Points in an Area

If there are multiple points close together in the area where you click, a pop-up menu is displayed. You can select one label for display from the pop-up menu. This selection also determines which case is highlighted in the Data Editor.

Labels

The type of label displayed depends on previous specifications. The value of the ID label is displayed if an ID or case label variable was specified when the chart was defined. In Figure 6.27, the labels are from the case label variable, *name*. It was specified when the scatterplot was defined, as shown in Figure 6.28.

Figure 6.28   Simple Scatterplot dialog box

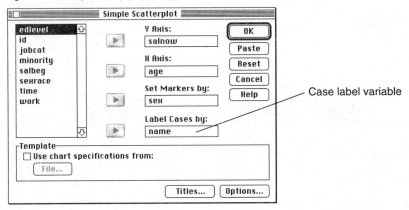

The case number is displayed if there is no ID or case label variable, as shown in Figure 6.29. Case numbers are also displayed if you have selected Case number in the Scatter-plot Options dialog box (see "Scatterplot Options: Simple and Matrix" on p. 129 in Chapter 7).

Figure 6.29   Case numbers in a scatterplot

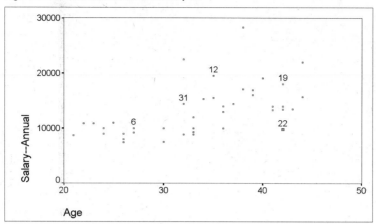

Locating a Case

If you select a point and then click on the Go to Data tool on the toolbar, the Data Editor becomes the active window, and the case that corresponds to the point selected on the chart is highlighted. Figure 6.30 shows a selected point, and Figure 6.31 shows the corresponding case highlighted in the Data Editor.

Figure 6.30   Scatterplot with a point selected

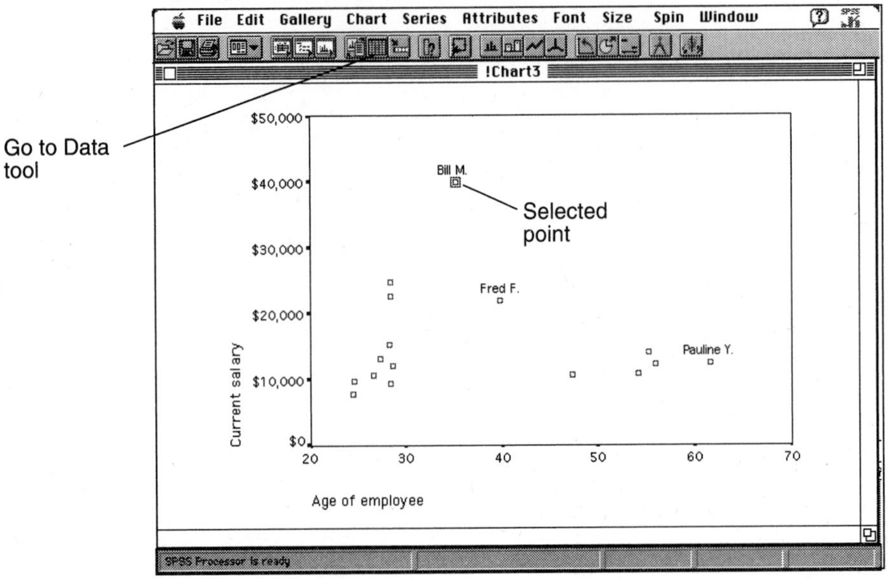

Go to Data tool

Selected point

Figure 6.31   Case highlighted in the Data Editor

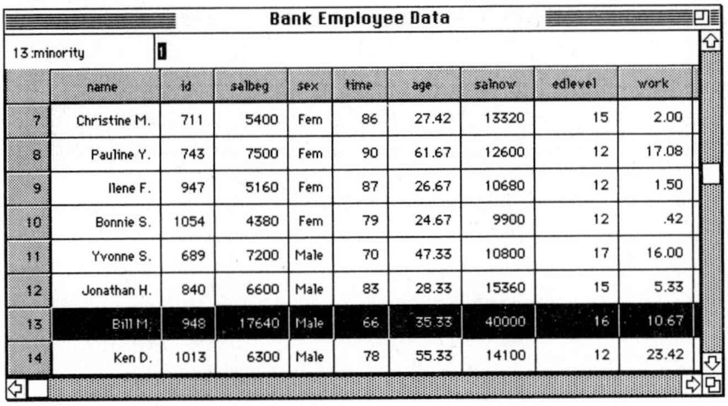

If you click on another unlabeled point in the scatterplot while in point selection mode, its label is turned on and the highlight in the Data Editor moves to the newly selected case.

Links between the Chart and the Data Editor

If you change the case structure of the data file or alter it in other ways, the link between the data file and the Data Editor is broken. The link is permanently broken when you do any of the following:

- Open a new file or a saved file.
- Transpose, merge, or aggregate the file.
- Read a matrix data file.
- Sort cases, using the options available in the Sort Cases dialog box and in several others, including the Split File dialog box.
- Insert a case anywhere but at the end of the working data file.
- Delete any case other than the last from the working data file. You can delete a case by cutting it or by running Select Cases from the Data menu.
- Replace or add variables.
- Open a saved chart.

If the link between the chart and the Data Editor is broken, any case selected is no longer highlighted in the Data Editor, and case numbers displayed as point labels refer to the case numbers in the original data file, as it was when the chart was created.

The Point Selection cursor has two shapes, depending on whether the link between the chart and the Data Editor is on or off. The shapes are shown in Figure 6.32.

Figure 6.32 Shapes of the Point Selection cursor

Links on   Links off

Finding a Case

If the link between the chart and the data file that created it has not been broken, you can click on a point in the chart (in point selection mode), and the corresponding case will be highlighted in the Data Editor.

If there is no link, you can label the point in the chart. If it is labeled with an ID or case label variable, you can go to the Data Editor, click in the column of the variable, and choose Search for Data from the Edit menu.

Spin for 3-D Scatterplots

Rotating a 3-D Chart

 If the current chart is a 3-D scatterplot, you can rotate in six directions. To rotate a 3-D scatterplot, click on the 3-D Rotation tool, or from the menus choose:

Spin
  3-D Rotation...

This opens the 3-D Rotation dialog box, as shown in Figure 6.33.

Figure 6.33   3-D Rotation dialog box

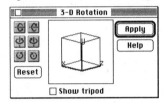

The direction of rotation is indicated on each button. Rotation is about one of three lines: a horizontal line in the plane of the screen, a vertical line in the plane of the screen, or a line perpendicular to the plane of the screen. You can click on a rotation button and release it, or you can click and hold the mouse button until you get as much rotation as you want. The rotation is illustrated in the center of the dialog box. When you have reached the orientation you want, click on Apply and then click on Close. Clicking on the Reset pushbutton returns the chart to the default orientation.

❑ **Show tripod.** Displays a tripod composed of lines parallel to the x, y, and z axes, with their intersection at the center of the wireframe.

Using Spin Mode

 For another way to rotate 3-D charts, click on the Spin Mode tool, or from the menus choose:

Spin
  Spin Mode

In this mode, the chart is stripped down for the duration of spinning. Only the tripod is shown and solid markers are hollow. The toolbar displays spin tools, as shown in Figure 6.34.

Figure 6.34   Spin tools

To rotate the chart in increments, click on one of the rotation tools. You can also click and hold a rotation tool while the chart spins.

Reset. Returns the chart to the default orientation.

Cancel. Ends spin mode and cancels any change in orientation.

Spin mode allows you to watch the pattern of the points change while you spin the chart. As in the other rotation mode, you can click on a rotation button and release it, or you can hold it down while the chart spins. When you are satisfied with the chart orientation, click on the Spin Mode tool again. The rotated chart is returned to the full version in the new position with its other attributes and options restored.

To increase the speed of spinning, you can reduce the screen area to be updated by changing the size of the window.

7

Modifying Chart Elements: Chart Menu

This chapter explains how to modify many of the elements of your chart by accessing dialog boxes available from the Chart menu.

From the Chart menu, you can:

- Alter the arrangement of the display or connect data points.
- Fit a variety of curves.
- Alter the scale, range, appearance, and labels of either axis, if appropriate.
- Adjust spacing between bars and between clusters of bars.
- Move the origin line in a bar chart to show how data values fall above and below the new origin line.
- Outside the chart itself, add or remove a one- or two-line title, a subtitle, and footnotes, any of which can be left- or right-justified or centered.
- Suppress or edit the legend.
- Add annotation text, at any position in the plot area, framed or unframed.
- Add horizontal and vertical reference lines.
- Swap axes.
- Explode one or more pie slices.
- Add or remove the inner frame or outer frame.
- Edit the color palette.

Accessing Chart Options

The Options dialog box appropriate to the type of chart is determined by the system. (Difference line charts have no specific options.) To access options, do one of the following:

- From the menus choose:

  Chart
    Options...

or

- Double-click in an area of the chart away from the chart objects.

or

- Click on the Options tool.

Bar/Line/Area Options

To change options for a bar, line, or area chart, from the menus choose:

Chart
  Options...

This opens the Bar/Line/Area Options dialog box, as shown in Figure 7.1.

Figure 7.1   Bar/Line/Area Options dialog box (bar chart active)

For bar or area charts, you can change the scale axis to percentage representation.

❏ **Change scale to 100%.** In a bar chart, this option automatically stacks the bars and changes each resulting bar to the same total length, representing 100% for the category (see Figure 7.2). In an area chart, the total distance from the axis, representing 100%, is the same for each category. This feature is useful for comparing the relative percentages of different categories.

Figure 7.2   Stacked and 100% bar charts

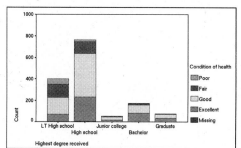
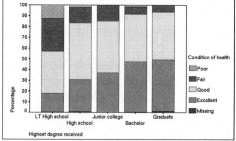

Line Options. Line options are available for line charts. You can choose one or both of the following options:

❏ **Connect markers within categories.** Applies to charts with more than one line. If this option is selected, vertical lines are drawn connecting the data points in the same category on different lines (different series). This option does not affect the current state of interpolation or line markers.

❏ **Display projection.** Select this option to differentiate visually between values to the left and values to the right in a line chart. To specify the category at which the projection begins, click on Location in the Bar/Line/Area Options dialog box. This opens the Projection dialog box, as shown in Figure 7.3.

Figure 7.3   Bar/Line/Area Options Projection dialog box

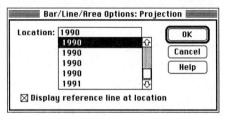

Choose the category where you want the projection line to start. The projection line will be displayed with a weight or style different from the original line. To make the projection stand out, you can select each part of the line individually and change its attributes. For example, the left part of the data line could be red and heavy while the right part of the data line, representing the projection, could be blue, thin, and dotted. An example is shown in Figure 7.4.

❏ **Display reference line at location.** Displays a line perpendicular to the category axis at the selected location.

Figure 7.4   Projection line chart

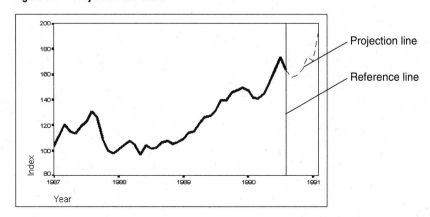

Bar Type. If two or more series are displayed in a bar chart, two bar types are available. You can choose one of the following options:

 Clustered. Bars are grouped in clusters by category. Each series has a different color or pattern, identified in the legend.

 Stacked. Bar segments, representing the series, are stacked one on top of the other for each category.

Pie Options

 To change options for a pie chart, from the menus choose:

Chart
  Options...

This opens the Pie Options dialog box, as shown in Figure 7.5.

Figure 7.5   Pie Options dialog box

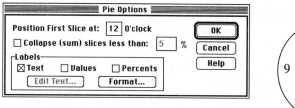 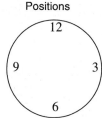

Position First Slice at n O'clock. Enter an integer from 1 to 12 to determine the position of the first sector or "slice" of the pie. The integers represent the positions of the hours on a clock face. The default position is 12.

To combine the smallest slices into one slice labeled *Other*, select the following option:

❑ **Collapse (sum) slices less than n%.** Adds the values of the summary functions of the smallest slices and displays the sum as one slice labeled *Other*. This formatting option does not recalculate any statistics and is appropriate only for functions that have a meaningful sum—that is, if you defined the summary function as N of cases, % of cases, Number of cases, Sum of values, Number above, Number below, or Number within.

If you select this option, each category for which the summary function has a value less than the specified percentage of the whole pie becomes part of the slice labeled *Other*. You can enter an integer from 0 to 100. If you create another chart type from the Gallery menu, all of the original categories are available.

Labels. You can choose one or more of the following label options. You can also control the format of labels. See "Label Format," below.

❏ **Text.** Displays a text label for each slice. To edit the labels, see "Edit Text Labels," below.

❏ **Values.** Displays the value of the summary function for each slice.

❏ **Percents.** Displays the percentage of the whole pie that each slice represents.

Edit Text Labels

To edit text labels, click on Edit Text in the Pie Options dialog box. This opens the Edit Text Labels dialog box, as shown in Figure 7.6.

Figure 7.6   Edit Text Labels dialog box

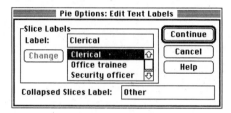

Slice Labels. To change the text of a slice label, select the label from the scroll list, edit it in the Label text box, and click on Change. Text labels can be up to 20 characters long.

Collapsed Slices Label. To change the text of collapsed slices label, edit it directly. (This label is available only if Collapse (sum) slices less than n% is selected in the Pie Options dialog box.)

When you have finished editing, click on Continue.

Label Format

To control the format of labels, click on Format in the Pie Options dialog box. This opens the Label Format dialog box, as shown in Figure 7.7. (You can also select the labels in the chart and change the color, font, and size attributes.)

Figure 7.7   Label Format dialog box

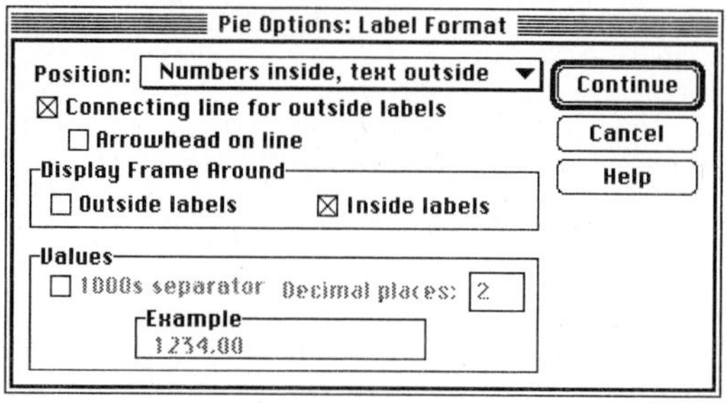

● **Position.** Places labels in relation to the pie. You can choose one of the following alternatives:

Outside, justified. Labels are placed outside the pie slices. Labels to the left of the pie are left-justified; labels to the right of the pie are right-justified.

Outside. Labels are placed outside the pie slices.

Inside. Labels are placed inside the pie slices.

Best fit. Labels are placed in the space available.

Numbers inside, text outside. Values and percentages are placed inside of the slices; their labels are placed outside of the slices.

Display Frame Around. Both inside and outside labels can have frames around them. You can select one or both sets of frames.

❑ **Outside labels.** Displays a frame around each label outside the pie.

❑ **Inside labels.** Displays a frame around each label within the pie.

Values. This group controls the format of displayed numbers. Your selections are displayed in the Example box.

❑ **1000s separator.** Displays values greater than 1000 with the separator (period or comma) currently in effect.

Decimal places. You can specify any number of decimal places from 0 to 19 for values. However, the number of decimal places will be truncated to fit within the 20-character limit for values. If you specify 0, percentages, if selected, will also have no decimal places. If you specify an integer from 1 to 19, percentages will be shown with one decimal place.

You can also choose the following option:

❏ **Connecting line for outside labels.** Displays a line connecting each outside label with the slice of the pie to which it applies.

  ❏ **Arrowhead on line.** Places arrowheads on connecting lines pointing to the slices. Arrowheads are not available if the position selected is Outside, justified.

Boxplot Options

To change options for a boxplot, double-click on one of the *n* values on the category axis, or from the menus choose:

Chart
  Options...

This opens the Boxplot Options dialog box, as shown in Figure 7.8.

Figure 7.8   Boxplot Options dialog box

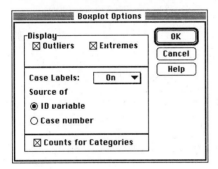

Display. Options in this group control whether outliers and extremes are shown in the chart. The height of the box is the interquartile range (IQR) computed from Tukey's hinges. You can choose one or more of the following alternatives:

❏ **Outliers.** Displays values that are more than 1.5 IQR's, but less than 3 IQR's, from the end of a box.

❏ **Extremes.** Displays values that are more than 3 IQR's from the end of a box.

Case Labels. Controls whether or not labels are displayed. You can choose one of the following alternatives:

⬇ **Off.** No labels are displayed.

  On. All points on the chart are labeled.

As is. Some points are labeled, as selected on the chart with the Point Selection tool. If you select As is after a previous selection of Off or On, no labels will be changed.

Source of Labels. When a boxplot is created, each point is associated with a case number in the working data file. A boxplot can also have a case label variable selected in the dialog box used to create the chart. If the chart has a case label variable, you can choose one of the following alternatives:

○ **ID variable.** Each label is the value of the case label variable for the case. This is the default if a case label variable was specified.

○ **Case number.** Each label is the value of the case number in the Data Editor.

The Case Labels group is available only if Outliers or Extremes is selected. If you deselect both Outliers and Extremes, the labels retain their current status. If either is turned back on, the labels will be displayed as they were when both were turned off.

You can also choose the following option:

❑ **Counts for categories.** Displays the number of cases under each category.

Error Bar Options

To change options for an error bar chart, double-click on one of the *n* values on the category axis, or from the menus choose:

Chart
  Options...

This opens the Error Bar Options dialog box, as shown in Figure 7.9.

Figure 7.9   Error Bar Options dialog box

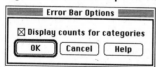

You can choose the following option:

❑ **Display counts for categories.** Displays the number of cases under each category. This option is selected by default.

Scatterplot Options: Simple and Matrix

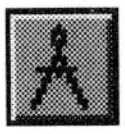

The options for a scatterplot vary according to the type of scatterplot—simple and matrix, overlay, or 3-D. To change options for a simple or matrix scatterplot, from the menus choose:

Chart
 Options...

This opens the Scatterplot Options dialog box for simple and matrix scatterplots, as shown in Figure 7.10.

Figure 7.10 Scatterplot Options dialog box for simple and matrix scatterplots

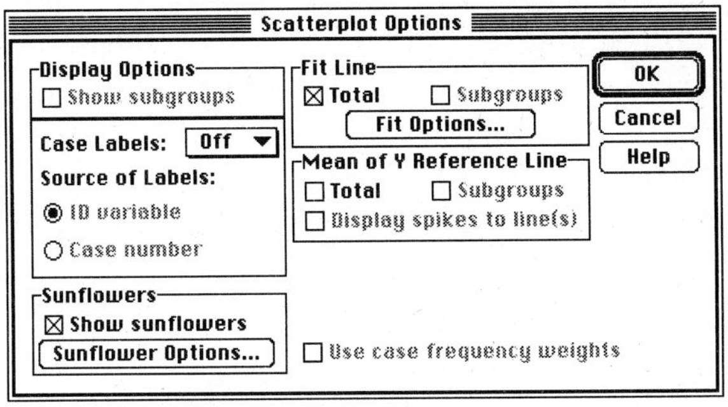

Display Options. Selected display options control how the groups and cases are differentiated. You can choose the following option:

❑ **Show subgroups.** If a control variable was defined using Set markers by, this option is selected and markers of different colors or styles are used to differentiate the groups defined by the control variable. This option must be selected for subgroup options in other dialog boxes to be enabled.

Case Labels. Controls whether or not labels are displayed. You can choose one of the following alternatives:

🠇 **Off.** No labels are displayed.

On. All points on the chart are labeled.

As is. Some points are labeled, as selected on the chart with the Point Selection tool. If you select As is after a previous selection of Off or On, no labels are changed.

Source of Labels. When scatterplots are created, each point is associated with a case number in the working data file. Many scatterplots also show an ID variable or a case label variable that was selected in the dialog box used to create the chart. If there is such a variable, you can choose one of the following alternatives:

○ **ID variable.** Each label is the value of the case label variable for the case. This is the default if a case label variable was specified.

○ **Case number.** Each label is the case number. Case numbers refer to the working data file at the time the chart was created.

Fit Line. Fit Line options add one or more lines or curves to the chart, showing the best fit according to the method you select for Fit Options (see "Fit Options" on p. 131). You can choose one or both of the following alternatives:

❑ **Total.** Fits the total set of data points.

❑ **Subgroups.** Fits the selected type of curve to each subgroup. This option is enabled only if subgroups are defined and shown.

Sunflowers. The Sunflowers option allows you to group the data points into two-dimensional cells in the chart, with a **sunflower** in each cell. The process is similar to grouping the values for one variable into bars on a histogram. The number of cases in a cell is represented by the number of petals on the sunflower. You can also customize the display of sunflowers. See "Sunflower Options" on p. 133.

❑ **Show sunflowers.** To represent the data as sunflowers, select this option.

Sunflowers and Labels. If labels are turned on, sunflowers are not displayed. If labels are turned off and sunflowers are selected, sunflowers are displayed.

Mean of Y Reference Line. You can draw a reference line through the y axis at the mean of all the y values and reference lines at the means of defined subgroups. If you have a scatterplot matrix, any items apply to each part of the matrix. You can choose one or more of the following alternatives:

❑ **Total.** Produces one line at the mean y value for all of the data points.

❑ **Subgroups.** Controls whether a line is shown for the mean of each subgroup. This option is available only if you specified a control variable to define subgroups and if Show subgroups is selected for Display Options.

❑ **Display spikes to line(s).** Produces a spike from each point to the appropriate mean reference line. If both Total and Subgroups are selected, spikes are drawn to the subgroup lines.

If you have defined a weight variable by selecting Weight Cases from the Data menu, the weights are automatically applied to a simple or overlay plot.

❑ **Use case frequency weights.** Selected by default if a weight variable was previously defined. (The SPSS status bar indicates Weight On.) When weight is on, a message appears in a footnote below the chart. Weighted values are used to compute fit lines, mean of y reference lines, confidence limits, intercept, R^2, and sunflowers.

Deselecting this option does not restore cases that were excluded from the chart because of missing or non-positive weights.

Fit Options

To select a method for fitting the points to a line, click on Fit Options in the Scatterplot Options dialog box. This opens the Fit Line dialog box, as shown in Figure 7.11.

Figure 7.11   Fit Line dialog box

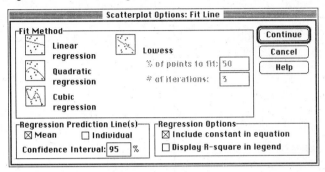

Fit Method. The picture buttons illustrate three regression types and another method for fitting the data points in a scatterplot. Examples of curves drawn by the fit methods are shown in Figure 7.12. You can choose one of the following options:

 Linear regression. Produces a linear regression line that best fits the data points on a scatterplot according to the least-squares principle. This is the default fit method.

 Quadratic regression. Produces a quadratic regression curve that best fits the data points on a scatterplot according to the least-squares principle.

 Cubic regression. Produces a cubic regression curve that best fits the data points on a scatterplot according to the least-squares principle.

 Lowess. Lowess uses an iterative weighted least-squares method to fit a line to a set of points. At least 13 data points are needed. This method fits a specified percentage of the data points. The default is 50%. It also uses a specified number of iterations. The default is 3.

Regression Prediction Line(s). Produces lines illustrating the confidence level that you specify. The default confidence level is 95%. These prediction lines are available only if one of the regression types is selected. You can choose one or both of the following alternatives:

❑ **Mean.** Plots the prediction intervals of the mean predicted responses.

❑ **Individual.** Plots the prediction intervals for single observations.

Confidence Interval. Specify a confidence level between 10.0 and 99.9. The default value is 95.

Regression Options. Available only if one of the regression types is selected. You can choose one or both of the following alternatives:

❑ **Include constant in equation.** Displays a regression line passing through the y intercept. If this option is deselected, the regression line passes through the origin.

❑ **Display R-squared in legend.** Displays the value of R^2 for each regression line in the legend, if it is displayed. This option is not available on matrix scatterplots. To display the legend, from the menus choose:

Chart
  Legend...

and select Display legend.

Figure 7.12   Examples of fit methods

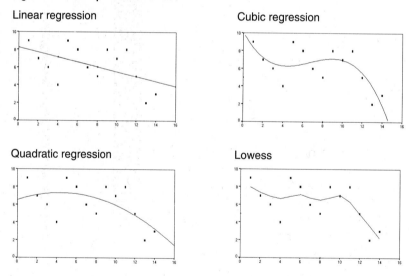

Linear regression

Cubic regression

Quadratic regression

Lowess

To access other methods of connecting the points in a scatterplot, from the menus choose:

Series
  Interpolation...

See "Line Interpolation" on p. 109 in Chapter 6 for more information.

Sunflower Options

To customize the display of sunflowers, click on Sunflower Options in the Scatterplot Options dialog box. This opens the Sunflowers dialog box, as shown in Figure 7.13.

Figure 7.13   Sunflowers dialog box

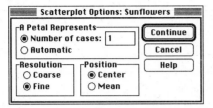

A Petal Represents. The petal number is equal to the number of cases in the cell (weighted or not) divided by the number of cases specified per petal. If the petal number is between 0 and 1.5, the center of the sunflower is displayed in the cell. If the petal number is 1.5 or greater, it is rounded, and the rounded number of petals is displayed. For example, in a nonweighted situation where each petal represents one case, a cell containing one case has only a sunflower center. A cell containing two cases has a sunflower with two petals, a cell with three cases has three petals, and so on.

You can choose one of the following alternatives:

○ **Number of cases.** Enter the number of cases per petal.

○ **Automatic.** The system determines the number of cases per petal automatically.

Resolution. Controls the size of the cells. You can choose one of the following alternatives:

○ **Coarse.** Plots cases from a large area on one sunflower. Each dimension of a sunflower cell is 1/8 of the appropriate range.

○ **Fine.** Plots cases from a small area on one sunflower. Each dimension of a sunflower cell is 1/15 of the appropriate range.

Position. Controls the placement of the sunflower within the cell. You can choose one of the following alternatives:

○ **Center.** Positions each sunflower in the center of its cell.

○ **Mean.** Positions each sunflower at the intersection of the means for the points in the cell.

Figure 7.14 contains examples of data plotted as a simple scatterplot and the same data displayed with sunflowers.

Figure 7.14   Sunflowers

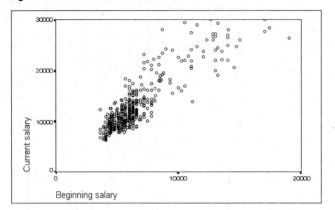

No sunflowers

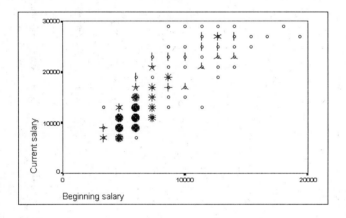

Sunflowers
(fine, center)

Overlay Scatterplot Options

To change options for an overlay scatterplot, from the menus choose:

Chart
  Options...

This opens the Overlay Scatterplot Options dialog box, as shown in Figure 7.15.

Figure 7.15   Overlay Scatterplot Options dialog box

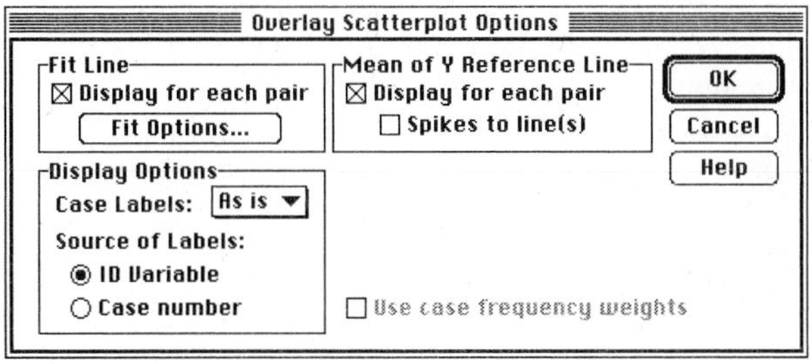

Fit Line. You can add lines or curves to the chart, showing the best fit.

❑ **Display for each pair.** If this item is selected, a line or curve is fitted for each pair of variables. To choose the type of line or curve, click on Fit Options to open the Fit Line dialog box, shown in Figure 7.11. Available options are described in "Fit Options" on p. 131.

Mean of Y Reference Line. You can request a line drawn at the mean of the *y* values.

❑ **Display for each pair.** Draws a separate reference line for each pair of variables.

    ❑ **Spikes to line(s).** Produces a spike from each point to the appropriate mean reference line. Spikes are available only if the reference lines are displayed for each pair.

Display Options. The following options apply to case labels.

Case Labels. Controls whether or not labels are displayed. You can choose one of the following alternatives:

◆ **Off.** No labels are displayed.

   On. All points on the chart are labeled.

   As is. Some points are labeled, as selected on the chart with the Point Selection tool. If you select As is after a previous selection of Off or On, no labels are changed.

Source of Labels. When scatterplots are created, each point is associated with a case number in the working data file. Many scatterplots also show an ID variable or a case label variable that was selected in the dialog box used to create the chart. If there is such a variable, you can choose one of the following alternatives:

○ **ID variable.** Each label is the value of the case label variable for the case. This is the default if a case label variable was specified.

○ **Case number.** Each label is a case number. Case numbers refer to the working data file at the time the chart was created.

You can also select the following option:

❑ **Use case frequency weights**. Selected by default if a weight variable was previously defined by selecting Weight Cases from the Data menu. (The status bar indicates Weight On.) When weighting is on, a message appears in a footnote below the chart. Weighted values are used to compute fit lines, mean of *y* reference lines, confidence limits, and intercepts. Deselecting this option does not restore cases that were excluded from the chart because of missing or non-positive weights.

3-D Scatterplot Options

To change options for a 3-D scatterplot, from the menus choose:

Chart
  Options...

This opens the 3-D Scatterplot Options dialog box, as shown in Figure 7.16.

Figure 7.16   3-D Scatterplot Options dialog box

```
═══════ 3-D Scatterplot Options ═══════
  ⊠ Show subgroups            ┌─────────┐
  Case Labels:   [ As is  ▼]  │   OK    │
  Source of Labels:           └─────────┘
  ◉ ID variable               ┌─────────┐
  ○ Case number               │ Cancel  │
                              └─────────┘
  ☐ Use case frequency weights ┌─────────┐
  Spikes: [  None    ▼]        │  Help   │
  ┌Wireframe────────┐          └─────────┘
  │ [⬡] [⬡]  [⋰]  │
  └─────────────────┘
```

You can choose the following option:

❑ **Show subgroups**. If a control variable was defined using Set markers by in the 3-D Scatterplot dialog box, markers of different colors or styles are used to differentiate the subgroups defined by the control variable.

Case Labels. Controls whether or not labels are displayed. You can choose one of the following alternatives:

⬥ **Off.** No labels are displayed.

On. All points on the chart are labeled.

As is. Some points are labeled, as selected on the chart with the Point Selection tool. If you select As is after a previous selection of Off or On, no labels are changed.

Source of Labels. When scatterplots are created, each point is associated with a case number in the working data file. Many scatterplots also show an ID variable or a case label variable that was selected in the dialog box used to create the chart. If there is such a variable, you can choose one of the following alternatives:

❍ **ID variable.** Each label is the value of the case label variable for the case. This is the default if a case label variable was specified.

❍ **Case number.** Each label is the case number. Case numbers refer to the working data file at the time the chart was created.

You can also choose the following option:

❑ **Use case frequency weights.** Selected by default if a weight variable was previously defined by selecting Weight Cases from the Data menu. (The status bar indicates Weight On.) When weighting is turned on, a message appears in a footnote below the chart. Weighted values are used to calculate the centroid. Deselecting this option does not restore cases that were excluded from the chart because of missing or nonpositive weights.

Spikes. Displays a line from each data point to the location that you specify. Spikes are especially useful when printing a 3-D scatterplot. You can choose one of the following alternatives:

◆ **None.** No spikes are displayed.

Floor. Spikes are dropped to the plane of the *x* and *z* axes of a 3-D scatterplot.

Origin. Spikes end at the origin (0,0,0). The origin may be outside of the display.

Centroid. Spikes are displayed from each point to the centroid of all the points. The coordinates of the centroid are the weighted means of the three variables. A missing value in any one of the three variables excludes the case from the calculation. Changing the scale does not affect the calculation of the centroid.

Wireframe. The wireframe option draws a frame around the 3-D scatterplot to help you interpret it. You can choose one of the following alternatives:

The full frame shows all of the edges of a cube surrounding the data points.

The half frame shows the orientation of the three axes and their planes. This is the default wireframe.

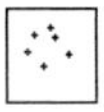
The cloud button allows you to suppress the wireframe entirely. You may want to use this view when rotating the cloud of points while looking for a pattern.

If you selected Spikes, the spikes are shown with or without a wireframe.

Histogram Options

To change options for a histogram, from the menus choose:

Chart
  Options...

This opens the Histogram Options dialog box, as shown in Figure 7.17.

Figure 7.17   Histogram Options dialog box

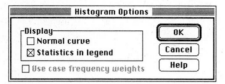

Display. You can choose one or both of the following display options:

❑ **Normal curve.** Superimposes a normal curve centered on the mean. The default histogram does not have a normal curve.

❑ **Statistics in legend.** Displays in the legend the standard deviation, the mean, and the number of cases. This item is selected by default. If you deselect the legend (see "Legends" on p. 154), the statistics display is also turned off.

The following option is also available:

❑ **Use case frequency weights.** Selected by default if a weight variable was previously defined by selecting Weight Cases from the Data menu. (The SPSS status bar indicates Weight On.) When weighting is on, a message appears in a footnote below the chart. Weighting affects the height of the bars and the computation of statistics. Deselecting this option does not restore cases that were excluded from the chart because of missing or non-positive weights. If the histogram was generated from the Frequencies procedure, the case weights cannot be turned off.

Axis Characteristics

You can modify, create, and change the orientation of axes in a chart. Axis dialog boxes can be opened in one of the following ways:

• Double-click near the axis.

or

• Select an axis or axis label and from the menus choose:

  Chart
    Axis...

  to open the appropriate (scale, category, or interval) axis dialog box.

or

• Without an axis selected, from the menus choose:

Chart
  Axis...

to open an Axis Selection dialog box, similar to the one shown in Figure 7.18. The types of axes represented in the current chart are listed in the dialog box. Select the type of axis you want to modify and click on OK.

Figure 7.18   Axis Selection dialog box showing scale and category axes

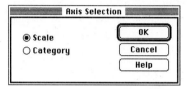

Scale Axis

If you select a scale axis, the Scale Axis dialog box appears, as shown in Figure 7.19.

Figure 7.19   Scale Axis dialog box

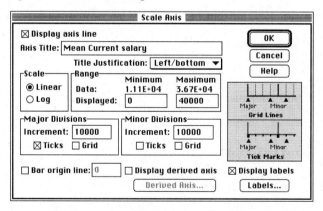

To display the axis line, select the following option:

❏ **Display axis line.** Controls the display of the axis line. Since it coincides with the inner frame, if you want no line displayed, you must also turn off the inner frame (see "Inner Frame" on p. 164). This item is not available for 3-D scatterplots.

Axis Title. You can type up to 72 characters for the axis title. To delete the title, delete all of the characters.

◆ **Title Justification.** Controls the position of the title relative to the axis. You can select one of the following alternatives:

Left/bottom. Axis title aligns to the left for horizontal axes and at the bottom for vertical axes.

Center. Axis title is centered (applies to both horizontal and vertical axes).

Right/top. Axis title aligns to the right for horizontal axes and at the top for vertical axes.

◆ **Title Orientation.** Available for 3-D scatterplots only. Controls the orientation of the title. You can select one of the following alternatives:

Horizontal. A horizontal title has one end near the center of the axis.

Parallel. A parallel title is parallel to the axis.

Scale. Controls whether the scale is linear or logarithmic. You can choose one of the following alternatives:

○ **Linear.** Displays a linear scale. This is the default.

○ **Log.** Displays a base 10 logarithmic scale. If you select this item, you can type new values for the range or you can click on OK and then click on Yes when the program asks if you want the default range. Logarithmic is not available for boxplots.

Range. Controls the displayed range of values. The minimum and maximum actual data values are listed for your information. If you change the range, you may also want to change the increments in Major Divisions and Minor Divisions.

If the scale is logarithmic, the range values are specified in the same units as the data values. The minimum must be greater than 0 and both values must be even logarithmic values (base 10)—that is, each must be an integer from 1 to 9 times a power of 10. For example, the range might be 9000 to 30000. If you enter unacceptable values and click on OK, the system asks if you want them adjusted.

Major Divisions/Minor Divisions. Allows you to control the marked increments along the axis. The number you enter for the increment must be positive and the range must be a multiple of the increment. The major increment must be a multiple of the minor increment. If the scale is logarithmic, you cannot change the increment.

❑ **Ticks**. If you do not want tick marks displayed, deselect this item.

❑ **Grid**. If you want grid lines displayed perpendicular to the axis, select this item.

The following option is available for bar charts:

❏ **Bar origin line.** Allows you to specify a location for the origin line from which bars will hang (vertical bars) or extend (horizontal bars). The specified value must fall within the current range. For example, two versions of a bar chart are shown in Figure 7.20, one with the origin line at 0 and the other with the origin line at 12,000. The second version emphasizes the differences in current salary for employees who have 16 or more years of education.

Figure 7.20   Bar origin lines

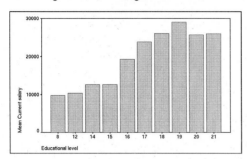 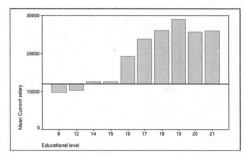

The following option allows you to display another scale opposite the original scale axis. It is selected by default in Pareto charts.

❏ **Display derived axis.** Allows you to specify an axis on the opposite side of the chart that has a different scale. In a Pareto chart, this axis commonly shows percentages. To specify the scale, title, increments, and labels, click on Derived Axis. This option is not available for histograms or scatterplots.

The following option is also available for most charts:

❏ **Display labels.** Allows you to suppress or display the labels on the original scale axis. To modify the labels, click on Labels. (See "Scale Axis Labels" on p. 144.)

Derived Scale Axis

The derived axis is opposite the original scale axis. To specify or change the details of the derived axis, click on Derived Axis in the Scale Axis dialog box. This opens the Scale Axis Derived Axis dialog box, as shown in Figure 7.21.

Figure 7.21   Scale Axis Derived Axis dialog box

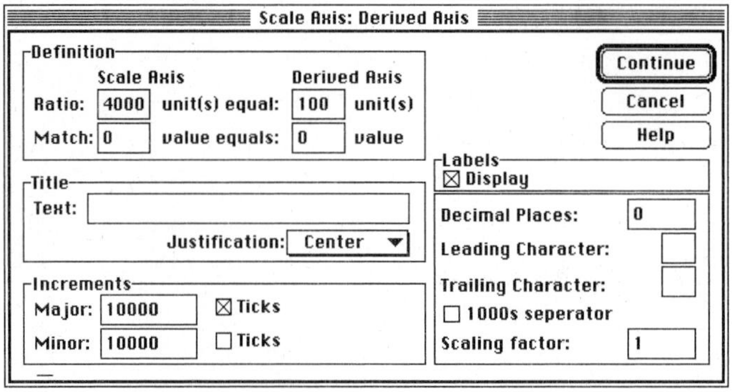

Definition. This group defines the derived axis in relation to the scale axis. The scale axis is not affected by these specifications.

Ratio: n unit(s) equal: n unit(s). The size of a unit on the derived axis is defined by its ratio to the size of a unit on the scale axis. In Figure 7.21, 100 units on the derived axis are the same size as 40,000 units on the scale axis (the text box has room to show only four digits). The numbers specified must be positive. When you have specified a ratio here, be sure to consider the size of increments near the bottom of this dialog box.

Match: n value equals: n value. Relates a specific position on the scale axis to a specific position on the derived axis. In Figure 7.21, the position of 0 on the scale axis matches the position of 0 on the derived axis. The match points do not have to be visible in the chart.

Title. The title is arranged so that it reads from top to bottom.

Text. The text of the title can be up to 72 characters. To delete the title, delete all of the characters.

◆ **Justification.** Controls the position of the title relative to the axis: top, center, or bottom. You can select one of the following alternatives:

Top. The derived axis title is aligned with the top of the axis. This is the default for a Pareto chart.

Center. The title is centered with respect to the axis.

Bottom. The end of the title is at the bottom of the axis.

Increments. Controls the definition and marking of increments along the derived axis. Increments should be considered in conjunction with the range displayed on this axis, which is determined by the definition of the ratio.

Major. These increments have labels if Display is selected in the Labels group in this dialog box. Major tick marks are emphasized when selected.

Minor. These increments do not have labels. If minor ticks are selected, the minor increment must divide evenly into the major increment.

The following option is available for the derived axis:

❏ **Display axis line.** Controls whether or not the axis line is displayed for the derived axis. If you want no line at this position, you must deselect the inner frame on the Chart menu.

Labels. The following options control the labels of the derived axis:

❏ **Display.** Controls the display of labels at major increments.

Decimal Places. Enter the number of digits you want displayed to the right of the decimal point. The number of decimal places is also applied to bar labels, if present.

Leading Character. Adds the specified character at the beginning of each axis label automatically. The most commonly used leading character is a currency symbol, such as the dollar sign ($).

Trailing Character. Adds the specified character to the end of each axis label automatically. The most commonly used trailing character is the percent sign (%).

To insert a thousands-digit separator in numeric axis labels, select the following option:

❏ **1000s separator.** Displays values greater than 1000 with the separator (period or comma) currently in effect.

Scaling Factor. Computes each label on the derived axis by dividing the original value by the scaling factor. For example, the labels 1,000,000, 2,000,000, etc., can be scaled to 1, 2, etc., and the word *millions* added to the axis title. The default value is 1. Bar labels, if present, are not affected.

Scale Axis Labels

To modify axis labels, click on Labels in the Scale Axis dialog box. This opens the Scale Axis Labels dialog box, as shown in Figure 7.22. Any changes you make are reflected in the Example box.

Figure 7.22   Scale Axis Labels dialog box

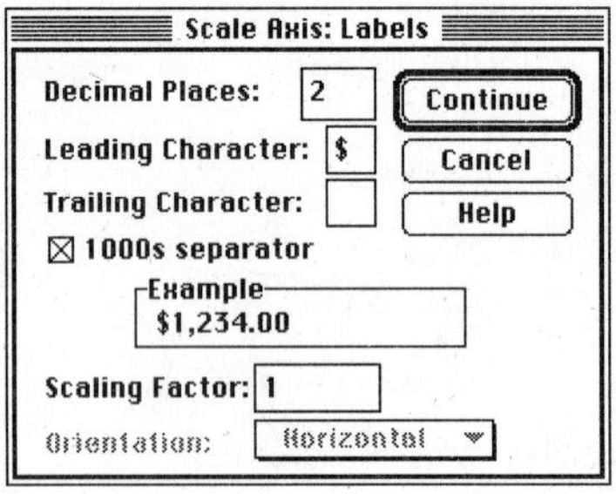

Decimal Places. Enter the number of digits you want displayed to the right of the decimal point. The number of decimal places is also applied to bar labels, if present.

Leading Character. Adds the specified character at the beginning of each axis label automatically. The most commonly used leading character is a currency symbol, such as the dollar sign ($).

Trailing Character. Adds the specified character to the end of each axis label automatically. The most commonly used trailing character is the percent sign (%).

To insert a thousands-digit separator in numeric axis labels, select the following option:

❑ **1000s separator.** Displays values greater than 1000 with the separator (period or comma) currently in effect.

Scaling Factor. Computes each label on the scale axis by dividing the original value by the scaling factor. For example, the labels 1,000,000, 2,000,000, etc., can be scaled to 1, 2, etc., and the word *millions* added to the axis title. The default value is 1. Bar labels, if present, are not affected.

Scatterplot Matrix Scale Axes

The dialog box for scatterplot matrix scale axes is shown in Figure 7.23. You can open the dialog box in one of the following ways:

- From the menus, choose:

  Chart
    Axis...

or

- Double-click on an axis.

or

- Double-click on one of the titles on the diagonal.

Figure 7.23   Scatterplot Matrix Scale Axes dialog box

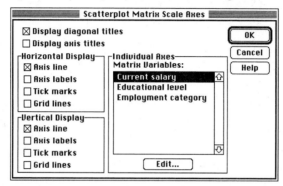

The options at the left in the dialog box apply to all of the plots in the matrix.

To display diagonal and axis titles, choose one or both of the following alternatives:

❏ **Display diagonal titles.** Displays titles on the diagonal of the matrix. Displayed by default.

❏ **Display axis titles.** Displays titles on the outer rim of the matrix.

Horizontal Display/Vertical Display. Items apply globally to all plots. Axis lines are displayed by default.

Individual Axes. Select one variable at a time and click on Edit to edit the selected axis. (See "Edit Selected Axis," below.)

Edit Selected Axis

To edit individual scatterplot matrix axes, click on Edit in the Scale Axes dialog box. This opens the Edit Selected Axis dialog box, as shown in Figure 7.24.

Figure 7.24   Edit Selected Axis dialog box

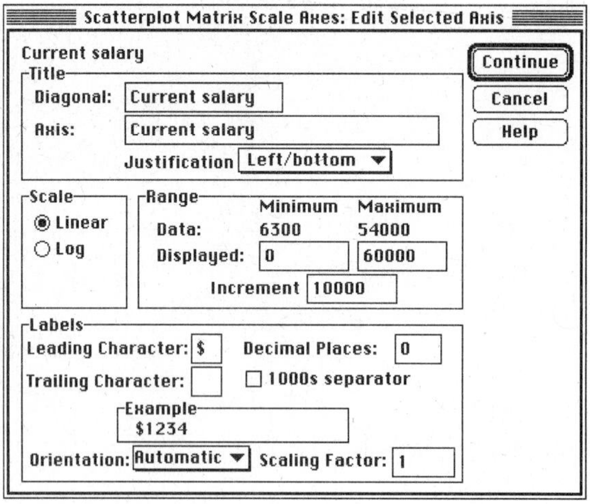

```
═════ Scatterplot Matrix Scale Axes: Edit Selected Axis ═════

 Current salary
 ┌Title───────────────────────────────────┐      ┌──────────┐
 │ Diagonal:  │ Current salary │           │      │ Continue │
 │                                         │      └──────────┘
 │ Axis:      │ Current salary       │     │      ┌──────────┐
 │                                         │      │  Cancel  │
 │      Justification │ Left/bottom  ▼ │   │      └──────────┘
 └─────────────────────────────────────────┘      ┌──────────┐
                                                   │   Help   │
 ┌Scale──┐┌Range──────────────────────────┐       └──────────┘
 │        ││          Minimum   Maximum    │
 │◉ Linear││  Data:     6300     54000     │
 │○ Log   ││  Displayed:│ 0 │   │ 60000 │  │
 │        ││                               │
 │        ││     Increment │ 10000 │       │
 └────────┘└───────────────────────────────┘

 ┌Labels──────────────────────────────────────┐
 │ Leading Character:│ $ │  Decimal Places:│ 0 │ │
 │                                             │
 │ Trailing Character:│  │  ☐ 1000s separator  │
 │           ┌Example────────────┐            │
 │           │ $1234             │            │
 │           └───────────────────┘            │
 │ Orientation:│ Automatic ▼ │ Scaling Factor:│ 1 │ │
 └─────────────────────────────────────────────┘
```

Title. Changes made to titles will be displayed only if you select the title display options in the Scale Axes dialog box. To fit titles into the space available, you can edit the text in the dialog box or select the text in the chart and change the size (see "Changing Text Objects" on p. 172 in Chapter 8).

> **Diagonal.** Allows you to edit the title that appears on the matrix diagonal.

> **Axis.** Allows you to edit the text of the axis title. With several plots in the matrix, the title for the axis often needs shortening.

> ➧ **Justification.** Controls the position of the title relative to the axis. You can select one of the following alternatives: Left/bottom, Center, or Right/top. Top and bottom apply to vertical axes. Left and right apply to horizontal axes. See "Axis Title" under "Scale Axis" on p. 139 for more information.

Scale. You can change the type of scale used for the axis.

○ **Linear.** Displays a linear scale. This is the default.

○ **Log.** Displays a logarithmic scale (base 10).

Range. Controls the displayed range of values.

> **Data.** The minimum and maximum actual data values are displayed for your information.

> **Displayed.** You can change the displayed range by typing the new minimum and maximum. The range must be an even multiple of the increment. If the scale is logarithmic, the range values are specified in the same units as the data values. The minimum

must be greater than 0 and both values must be even logarithmic values (base 10)—that is, the values of minimum and maximum must each be an integer from 1 to 9 times a power of 10. For example, a range could be 9000 to 30000. If you enter an unacceptable value, when you click on OK, the system asks if you want the values adjusted.

Increment. The value of the increment must divide evenly into the range.

Labels. The Labels group is available only if you selected Axis labels in either Horizontal Display or Vertical Display in the Scale Axes dialog box. Any changes you make are illustrated in the Example box.

Leading Character. Adds the specified character at the start of each axis label automatically. The most common leading character is a currency symbol, such as the dollar sign ($).

Trailing Character. Adds the specified character to the end of each axis label automatically. The most commonly used trailing character is the percent sign (%).

Decimal Places. Enter the number of digits you want displayed to the right of the decimal point.

❑ **1000s separator.** Displays values greater than 1000 with the separator (period or comma) currently in effect.

➥ **Orientation.** Controls the orientation of axis labels. Available only for a horizontal axis. You can select one of the following alternatives: Automatic, Horizontal, Vertical, Staggered, or Diagonal.

Scaling Factor. You can enter up to 20 characters in the box. The system divides each label by the factor. For example, the labels 1,000,000, 2,000,000, etc., can be scaled to 1, 2, etc., and the word *millions* added to the axis title. The default value is 1.

Category Axis

Selecting a category axis opens the Category Axis dialog box, as shown in Figure 7.25.

Figure 7.25   Category Axis dialog box

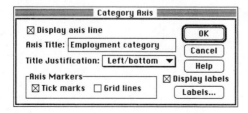

To display the category axis, select this option:

❏ **Display axis line.** Controls display of the axis line. Since it coincides with the inner frame, if you want no line displayed, you must also turn off the inner frame (see "Inner Frame" on p. 164).

Axis Title. You can type up to 72 characters for the axis title. To omit the title, delete all of the characters.

◆ **Title Justification.** Controls the position of the title relative to the axis. You can select one of the following alternatives: Left/bottom, Center, or Right/top. Top and bottom apply to vertical axes. Left and right apply to horizontal axes. See "Axis Title" under "Scale Axis" on p. 139 for more information.

Axis Markers. Controls whether tick marks and grid lines are turned on or off. You can choose one or both of the following alternatives:

❏ **Tick marks.** Controls the display of the tick marks for all categories. Tick marks are at the centers of the intervals.

❏ **Grid lines.** Controls the display of grid lines. Grid lines are at the bounds of intervals.

The following option is also available:

❏ **Display labels.** To display axis labels, select this option.

Category Axis Labels

To modify axis labels, click on Labels in the Category Axis dialog box. This opens the Category Axis Labels dialog box, as shown in Figure 7.26.

Figure 7.26   Category Axis Labels dialog box

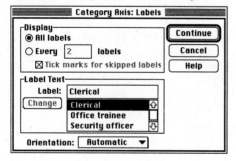

Display. Controls the display of axis labels. You can choose one of the following alternatives:

○ **All labels.** Displays a label for every category included in the display. To omit entire categories from the display, see "Bar, Line, and Area Chart Displayed Data" on p. 98 in Chapter 6.

○ **Every n labels.** Allows you to specify an increment governing the number of categories not labeled between displayed labels. Enter an integer that is 1 greater than the number of labels to be skipped. For example, if you want to label the first category, skip the next two, and label the fourth, enter 3.

  ❏ **Tick marks for skipped labels.** To turn off tick marks, deselect this option.

Label Text. Allows you to edit the text of labels. First select a label from the scroll list. It appears in the Label text box. Edit the text and click on Change.

➡ **Orientation.** Controls the orientation of axis labels. Available only for a horizontal category axis. You can select one of the following alternatives: Automatic, Horizontal, Vertical, Staggered, or Diagonal. See "Orientation" under "Scale Axis Labels" on p. 144 for more information.

Interval Axis

The bars of a histogram extend from an interval axis. The Interval Axis dialog box is shown in Figure 7.27.

Figure 7.27   Interval Axis dialog box

To display an axis line, select the following option:

❏ **Display axis line.** Controls display of the axis line. Since it coincides with the inner frame, if you want no line displayed, you must also turn off the inner frame (see "Inner Frame" on p. 164).

Axis Title. You can type up to 72 characters for the axis title. To omit the title, delete all the characters.

➡ **Title Justification.** Controls the position of the title relative to the axis. You can select one of the following alternatives: Left/bottom, Center, or Right/top. Top and bottom apply to vertical axes. Left and right apply to horizontal axes. Justification is with respect to the ends of the displayed axis. See "Axis Title" under "Scale Axis" on p. 139 for more information.

Axis Markers. Controls whether tick marks and grid lines are turned on or off. You can choose one or both of the following alternatives:

❑ **Tick marks.** Controls the display of the tick marks for all categories. Tick marks are at the centers of the intervals.

❑ **Grid lines.** Controls the display of grid lines. Grid lines are at the bounds of intervals.

Intervals. Allows you to define the size of the intervals represented by the bars in the histogram. You can choose one of the following alternatives:

○ **Automatic.** The number and size of intervals are determined automatically, based on your data. This is the default.

○ **Custom.** Allows you to define the size of equal intervals. Click on Define to change the number of intervals, the width of each interval, or the range of data displayed. See "Defining Custom Intervals," below.

The following display option is also available:

❑ **Display labels.** To display axis labels, select this option.

Defining Custom Intervals

To modify the number or width of intervals in a histogram, select Custom in the Interval Axis dialog box and click on Define to open the Define Custom Intervals dialog box, as shown in Figure 7.28.

Figure 7.28   Interval Axis Define Custom Intervals dialog box

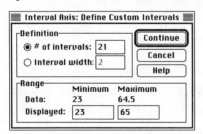

Definition. Two methods of specifying custom intervals are available. You can choose one of the following alternatives:

○ **# of intervals.** You can specify the number of intervals by entering an integer greater than 1. The system calculates the width of each interval, based on the range.

○ **Interval width.** You can enter a width for each interval, starting at the minimum listed under Range. The system calculates the number of intervals, based on the range.

Range. Allows you to adjust the range of data displayed. The minimum and maximum data values are listed for your information. You can adjust the range when you change the number of intervals or the interval width. For example, if you specify 10 intervals and a range of 20 to 70, the intervals start at 20 and are 5 units wide. (See Figure 7.29.) You can get the same result by specifying 5 as the interval width, along with the range of 20 to 70.

Figure 7.29   Histogram with custom intervals

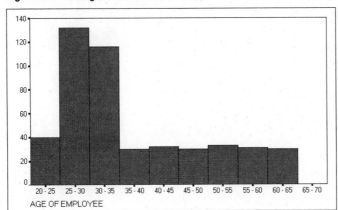

Modifying Interval Labels

Labels on an interval axis can be suppressed or modified. To modify the labels on the interval axis, click on Labels in the Interval Axis dialog box. This opens the Interval Axis Labels dialog box, as shown in Figure 7.30. Any changes you make are illustrated in the Example box.

Figure 7.30   Interval Axis Labels dialog box

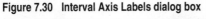
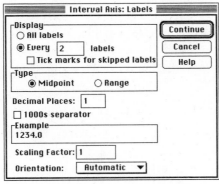

Display. Controls the display of axis labels.

○ **All labels.** Displays a label for every interval included in the display.

○ **Every n labels.** Allows you to specify an increment governing the number of intervals not labeled between displayed labels. Enter an integer that is 1 greater than the number of labels to be skipped. For example, if you want to label the first interval, skip the next two, and label the fourth, enter 3.

❑ **Tick marks for skipped labels.** To turn off tick marks, deselect this option.

Type. Allows you to select whether each label will denote the midpoint or the range of the interval.

○ **Midpoint.** Displays the midpoint of each interval as the label.

○ **Range.** Displays the lower and upper bounds of each interval as the label.

Decimal Places. You can specify the number of decimal places. Enter a value from 0 to 19.

To insert a thousands-digit separator in numeric axis labels, select the following option:

❑ **1000s separator.** Displays values greater than 1000 with the separator (period or comma) currently in effect.

Scaling Factor. You can enter up to 20 characters. The system divides each label by the factor. For example, the labels 1,000,000, 2,000,000, etc., can be scaled to 1, 2, etc., and the word *millions* added to the axis title. This factor does not affect the scale axis or bar labels.

◆ **Orientation.** Controls the orientation of axis labels. Available only for a horizontal axis. You can select one of the following alternatives: Automatic, Horizontal, Vertical, Diagonal, or Staggered.

Adding or Changing Explanatory Text

Explanatory text can be added to charts in the form of titles, footnotes, a legend, and text annotation.

Titles

To add a title to the top of a chart, from the menus choose:

Chart
　Title...

This opens the Titles dialog box, as shown in Figure 7.31. If you already have a title for the chart, you can double-click on it to open the dialog box.

Figure 7.31   Titles dialog box

```
┌═══════════════════ Titles ═══════════════════┐
│                                               │
│  Title 1: │Bank employees          │  ┌──────┐│
│  Title 2: │                        │  │  OK  ││
│                                       └──────┘│
│           Title Justification: │ Left  ▼│┌────────┐│
│                                         │ Cancel ││
│  Subtitle: │Work experience        │   └────────┘│
│           Subtitle Justification: │ Left ▼│┌──────┐│
│                                            │ Help ││
│                                            └──────┘│
└───────────────────────────────────────────────┘
```

Title 1/Title 2. You can enter up to 72 characters for each title. The amount of the title that is displayed depends on the length of the title and the size of the type font selected.

⬇ **Title Justification.** Both titles are justified together. You can choose one of the following alternatives: Left, Center, or Right. Left aligns the first character with the axis on the left; right aligns the last character with the right side of the inner frame.

Subtitle. You can enter up to 72 characters for the subtitle.

⬇ **Subtitle Justification.** A subtitle can be left- or right-justified or centered, independent of titles 1 and 2. The default font size for the subtitle is smaller than the font size for titles 1 and 2. You can choose one of the following alternatives: Left, Center, or Right.

To delete any title, delete all of the characters in its text.

Footnotes

To add up to two footnotes to a chart, from the menus choose:

Chart
  Footnote...

This opens the Footnotes dialog box, as shown in Figure 7.32. If you already have a footnote, you can double-click on it to open the dialog box.

Figure 7.32   Footnotes dialog box

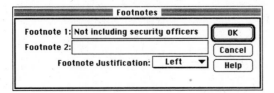

Footnote 1/Footnote 2. You can enter up to 72 characters for each footnote. The portion of a footnote that is displayed depends on the length of the footnote and the size of the type font selected.

✦ **Footnote Justification.** Footnotes are justified relative to the inner frame. You can choose one of the following alternatives: Left, Center, or Right. Left aligns the first character with the axis on the left; right aligns the last character with the right side of the inner frame. See "Axis Title" under "Scale Axis" on p. 139 for more information about justification.

To delete a footnote, delete all of the characters in its text.

Legends

If you have more than one series in a chart, the system provides a legend to distinguish between the series. A legend is also displayed automatically if you have statistics displayed for a histogram or R^2 for a regression line in a scatterplot. To make changes to the legend, double-click on the legend or from the menus choose:

Chart
  Legend...

This opens the Legend dialog box, as shown in Figure 7.33. The legend resulting from the specifications is shown in Figure 7.34.

Figure 7.33   Legend dialog box

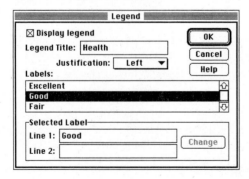

Figure 7.34   Legend example

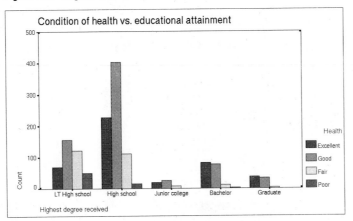

To display a legend for your chart, select the following option:

❑ **Display legend.** Controls whether the legend is displayed.

Legend Title. You can edit the legend title or add one if none exists. The legend title can be up to 20 characters long.

➥ **Justification.** Aligns the legend title within the area occupied by the legend. You can choose one of the following alternatives: Left, Center, or Right.

Labels. The labels in the legend are listed. When you select one of the labels from the list, it appears starting in Line 1 of the Selected Label group. You can edit the text and add a second line if it is not already there. Each line can be up to 20 characters long. When you have finished editing the label, click on Change.

Annotation

Annotation places text within the chart area, anchored to a specific point within the chart. To add annotation to the chart or edit existing annotation, from the menus choose:

Chart
   Annotation...

This opens the Annotation dialog box, as shown in Figure 7.35. The annotations resulting from these specifications are shown in Figure 7.36.

Figure 7.35   Annotation dialog box

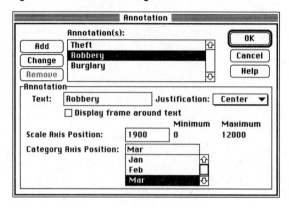

Figure 7.36   Annotation example

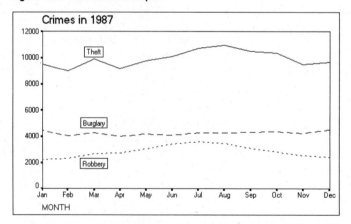

If you already have an annotation in the chart, you can edit it or add others by double-clicking on it. Since you position annotations at axis coordinates, the form of the Annotation dialog box depends on the kind of axes in your chart. Figure 7.35 shows an annotation dialog box for a chart containing a scale axis and a category axis.

For a new annotation, when the text and coordinates have been specified, click on Add and then on OK. To make changes to an existing annotation, select the annotation on the Annotation(s) list, edit the text or position, and click on Change.

Annotation. The default position for annotation is the intersection of the displayed axes (the lower left corner).

Text. Type up to 20 characters in the Text box.

⬇ **Justification.** The choices available on the drop-down list are Left, Center, or Right. The default is left, indicating that the leftmost character of the annotation will be positioned at the selected coordinates. In Figure 7.36, the annotations are *centered* above the tick mark for Mar.

❏ **Display frame around text.** Adds a frame around the annotation text.

Scale Axis Position. The scale axis position is a number between the minimum and maximum values.

Category Axis Position. If you have a category axis, the annotation will be positioned at the category you select from the scroll list. In Figure 7.36, all annotations are positioned at the category Mar, which makes them appear directly above one another.

Bar Styles

To add a drop shadow or a 3-D effect to a bar chart or a range bar chart, click on the Bar Style tool, or from the menus choose:

Chart
  Bar Style...

This opens the Bar Styles palette, as shown in Figure 7.37. Bars for every series in a chart have the same bar style.

Figure 7.37   Bar Styles palette

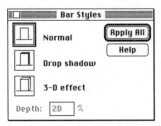

Normal. No shadows or 3-D effect. This is the default.

Drop shadow. Displays a shadow behind each bar. You can specify the depth of the shadow as a positive or negative percentage of the width of each original bar. The default is 20%. Positive depth places the shadow to the right of the bar; negative, to the left.

3-D effect. Displays each bar as a rectangular solid. You can specify depth as a percentage of the width of each original bar. The default is 20%. Switching from positive to negative depth changes the perspective of the viewer. With a positive value, you see the tops and right sides of the bars. With a negative value, you see the left sides.

If you have already changed the color or pattern of the original bars, the new block surfaces are displayed in the *default color and pattern*, while the front surface retains the attributes you selected previously. Once the shadows or 3-D bars are displayed, you can change the color and pattern of each type of individual surface, including the shadows or the side and top surfaces for each series.

Bar Label Styles

To label with its numerical value, each bar in a bar chart, range bar chart, or histogram, click on the Bar Label Style tool, or from the menus choose:

Chart
  Bar Label Style...

This opens the Bar Label Styles palette, as shown in Figure 7.38.

Figure 7.38   **Bar Label Styles palette**

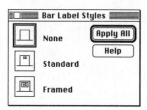

The bar label style applies to all of the bars in the chart. In a bar chart, the number of decimal places in the bar labels is the same as the number of decimal places in the scale axis labels.

None. No values appear on the bars. This is the default.

Standard. Displays a value at the top of each bar. It may or may not be easy to read, depending on the color and pattern of the bar. You can change the color, font, or size of the value text.

Framed. Displays the values in white frames at the tops of the bars. You can change the color, font, or size of the value text and the color of the frames.

Bar Spacing

To adjust the spacing of the bars in a bar chart, error bar chart, high-low-close chart, range bar chart, or histogram, from the menus choose:

Chart
  Bar Spacing...

The Bar Spacing dialog box for a bar chart is shown in Figure 7.39.

In a bar chart, you can change the margin spacing at both ends of the series of bars, the inter-bar spacing, and the inter-cluster spacing. The system adjusts the size of the bars to meet the new specifications.

For a histogram, the Bar Spacing dialog box contains only the bar margin specification.

Figure 7.39 Bar Spacing dialog box (bar chart)

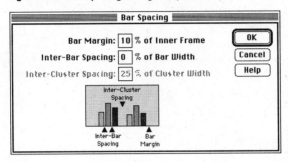

Bar Margin. The percentage (0 to 99) of the inner frame left blank on both sides of the series of bars. This percentage is split equally between the two sides. The default is 10% for bar charts and 0% for histograms.

Inter-Bar Spacing. The distance between bars within a cluster or the distance between bars in a simple bar chart. Enter the percentage of the bar width (0 to 100) that you want left blank between bars. The default is 0% for a clustered bar chart or 20% for a simple bar chart.

Inter-Cluster Spacing. The distance between clusters. Enter the percentage of the cluster width (0 to 100). The default is 25%.

Adding Reference Lines

To add one or more horizontal and vertical reference lines, from the menus choose:

Chart
  Reference Line...

This opens an Axis Selection dialog box appropriate for your chart. Dialog boxes for Category Axis Reference Lines and Scale Axis Reference Lines are shown in Figure 7.40 and Figure 7.41. The dialog box for Interval Axis Reference Lines is similar to the dialog box for Scale Axis Reference Lines.

Figure 7.40   Category Axis Reference Lines dialog box

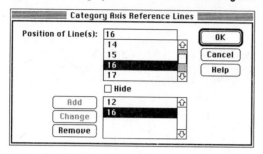

Figure 7.41   Scale Axis Reference Lines dialog box

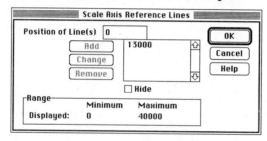

If you already have a reference line in the chart, you can open the dialog box to edit it or add other parallel reference lines by double-clicking on the line.

Position of Line(s). For a category axis, to add a new reference line, select one of the available categories and click on Add. The category is added to the list.

For a scale axis or interval axis, to add a new reference line, type a value and click on Add. The value is added to the list. If you type a value outside the displayed range, a warning message is displayed.

To remove a reference line, highlight it on the list and click on Remove. To change the position of a line, highlight it on the list, select a category or type a new value, and click on Change.

❏ **Hide.** Select this option to hide the reference line that is currently highlighted on the list. Then click on Add or Change. To display a previously hidden reference line, highlight it on the list, deselect Hide, and click on Change.

Figure 7.42 shows a chart that has one reference line perpendicular to the scale axis and two reference lines perpendicular to the category axis, as specified in the dialog boxes in Figure 7.40 and Figure 7.41.

Figure 7.42   Reference lines

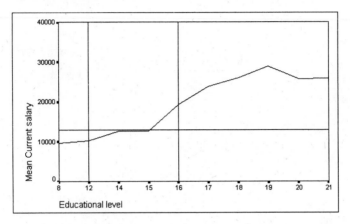

Swapping Axes in Two-Dimensional Charts

Category Charts and Histograms. In a 2-D bar chart, line chart, area chart, mixed chart, boxplot, or high-low chart with one scale axis, you can swap the axes. Swapping axes changes the orientation between vertical and horizontal. The bars, lines, or areas still represent the same values.

This is different from transposing, where the categories change places with the series named in the legend (see "Transposing Data" on p. 108 in Chapter 6). The difference between swapping axes and transposing data is illustrated in Figure 7.43.

Figure 7.43   Swapping axes and transposing data

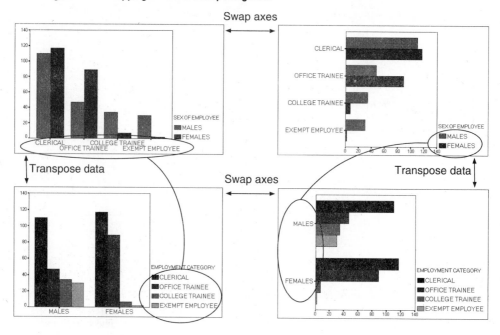

 To swap axes, click on the Swap Axes tool, or from the menus choose:

Chart
 Swap Axes

You can also use this procedure for boxplots and histograms.

Scatterplots. To swap the axes on a scatterplot, from the menus choose:

Series
 Displayed...

and assign the variables to different axes, as described in "Simple Scatterplot Displayed Data" on p. 104 in Chapter 6.

Exploding Pie Chart Slices

 You can **explode** (separate) one or more slices from a pie chart for emphasis (see Figure 7.44).

Figure 7.44   Pie chart with exploded slice selected

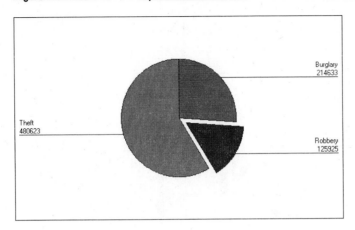

To explode a slice, select it and click on the Explode Slice tool, or from the menus choose:

Chart
  Explode Slice

To reverse the explosion, select the slice and click on the tool or menu choice again. A check mark on the menu indicates that the currently selected slice is exploded. You can explode two or more slices, one at a time.

To explode the whole pie, from the menus choose:

Gallery
  Pie...

and then click on Exploded.

Inner and Outer Frames

A chart has an inner frame and an outer frame. You can select either one by clicking on it, and you can change its attributes. If you want a fill color within a selected frame, be sure that the selection in the Fill Pattern dialog box is a pattern other than empty. Both frames are displayed in Figure 7.45. To set the default display for either frame, from the menus choose:

Edit
  Preferences...

and click on Graphics.

Figure 7.45 Inner and outer frames

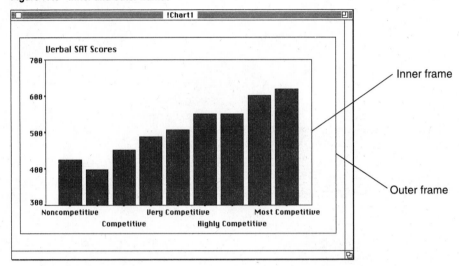

Inner Frame

The inner frame completes a rectangle, two sides of which coincide with the two axes. For most charts, the inner frame is displayed by default. To suppress or display the inner frame, from the menus choose:

Chart
  Inner Frame

When it is displayed, a check mark appears to the left of Inner Frame on the Chart menu.

Outer Frame

The outer frame encloses the titles, footnotes, and legend, as well as the chart. To display or suppress the outer frame, from the menus choose:

Chart
  Outer Frame

When it is displayed, a check mark appears to the left of Outer Frame on the Chart menu.

Refreshing the Screen

If your chart does not redraw correctly after you change the size of its window, from the menus choose:

Chart
  Refresh

The chart will be redrawn with the correct proportions.

Edit Colors

You can edit the colors available in the color table for the active chart or in the default color table which applies to any new charts. The color table is available from the Attributes menu when you select Fill color or Border color. To edit the color table, from the menus choose:

Chart
  Edit Colors

This opens the Edit Colors dialog box, as shown in Figure 7.46.

Figure 7.46   Edit Colors dialog box

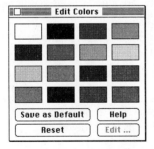

The dialog box contains 16 color swatches, indicating the colors that can be applied to chart objects. The color of a chart object is associated with a position in the palette; the chart object takes on whatever color is assigned to the swatch at that position.

Edit. Opens the color picker to change the color of the currently selected swatch. (See "Color Selection," below.) You cannot change the color of the black or white swatches.

Reset. Restores the default colors of all the swatches. Clicking on reset also changes the colors of elements in the chart to match the ones in the default palette.

Save as Default. Saves the current set of colors as the default. They will be used in creating new charts. Also, whenever you click on Reset, the swatches return to the default setting and colors of chart objects change to match their associated positions in the palette.

Color Selection

To assign custom colors, select a swatch in the Edit Colors dialog box, and click on Edit. The opens the Macintosh Standard Color Picker, as shown in Figure 7.47.

Figure 7.47   Macintosh Standard Color Picker

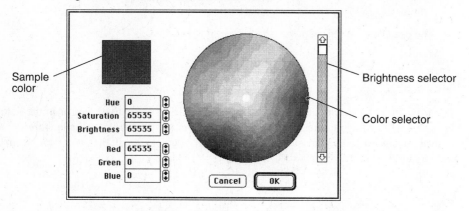

To change the color, you can use one of three methods:

- Use the mouse to move the color selector anywhere in the circle and to move the brightness selector up and down

- Use the arrows to change the Hue, Saturation, and Brightness or to change Red, Green, and Blue.

- Type numbers for Hue, Saturation, and Brightness or for Red, Green, and Blue. You can use numbers from 0 through 65535.

When the sample color is satisfactory, click on OK. The selected swatch in the Edit Colors dialog box changes, as do the chart objects associated with that swatch.

8 Modifying Chart Attributes: Attributes, Font, and Size Menus

The objects that make up a chart have attributes that can be modified:

- Almost all objects have color.
- Lines, including data lines, axes, and the borders surrounding areas, have style and weight.
- Areas have fill pattern.
- Markers have type (shape) and size.
- Text objects have font and size.

With the mouse, you select an object to modify and then make selections from palettes or menus (see "Selecting Objects to Modify" on p. 92 in Chapter 6).

Attributes menu. You can tear off and drag the Attributes utility window anywhere on the screen.

Palettes

When you select an item from the Attributes utility window, a palette opens. It contains swatches illustrating the patterns or styles available for the selected chart object.

- The pattern or style of the selected chart object is highlighted by a box drawn around a swatch.
- If you click on a swatch, the pattern or style is applied to the currently selected series or object.

Fill Color

Fill specifies the color inside the object if it is an area, or the color of other objects such as lines, markers, or text. To change the color of an object, select the object you want to change and from the menus choose:

Attributes
  Fill Color...

This opens the Colors palette, as shown in Figure 8.1.

Figure 8.1   Colors palette

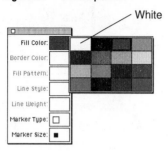

Drag the pointer to the color you want and release it. When you release the mouse button, the selected chart object changes to the color at the selected position in the palette.

The color of a chart object is associated with a position in the palette and takes on whatever color is currently in that position. For information on how to edit the colors on the palette, see "Edit Colors" on p. 165 in Chapter 7.

Border Color

Border color specifies the color of the border of an enclosed area. To change the border color, select an area in the chart, and from the menus choose:

Attributes
  Border Color...

This opens a colors palette, as shown in Figure 8.2.

Figure 8.2   Colors palette for border color

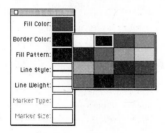

Drag the pointer to the color you want and release it. When you release the mouse button on a swatch in the palette, the color of the border of the selected area changes.

Fill Patterns

To change the pattern that is displayed in an enclosed area such as a bar series, the area under a line, or a background area, select the area and from the menus choose:

Attributes
 Fill Pattern...

This opens the Fill Patterns palette, as shown in Figure 8.3.

Figure 8.3   Fill Patterns palette

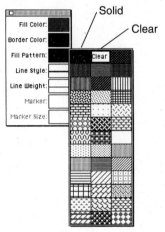

When you release the mouse button, the selected chart object changes to the selected pattern. You can use a fill pattern to make distinctions between the areas, especially if the chart is to be presented in black and white or a limited number of colors. In the palette itself, patterns appear in only one color, but your pattern selection is applied to whatever color is in the selected area.

The white picture button represents a clear area. If this fill pattern is selected, the selected object will appear white or have the same color as the background, no matter what color is selected in the Colors palette.

If the bar style is drop-shadow or 3-D effect, you can select any surface of a series of bars and change the fill pattern. For example, you can select the top surface of the 3-D bars for one pattern and the right side for another pattern.

Line Style

The lines in a chart, including the data lines and the axes, can have different styles. To change the style of a line, select it and from the menus choose:

Attributes
 Line Style

This opens the Line Style palette, as shown in Figure 8.4.

Figure 8.4   Line Style palette

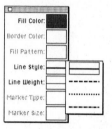

Drag the pointer to the style you want and release it. When you release the mouse button, the selected line changes to the selected style. The default is a solid line.

Line Weight

To change the thickness of a line, select it and from the menus choose:

Attributes
 Line Weight

This opens the Line Weight palette, as shown in Figure 8.5.

Figure 8.5   Line Weight palette

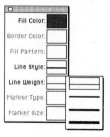

Drag the pointer to the weight you want and release it. When you release the mouse button, the selected line changes to the selected weight. The default is thin.

Markers

Markers are used to indicate the location of data points in a line chart, area chart, or scatterplot, and the data points for the close series in a high-low-close chart. By default, each series in a chart appears with a different color or with a different marker type, according to how your graphic preferences are set. If you have a line chart in which the markers are not displayed, open the Line Interpolation palette (see "Line Interpolation" on p. 109 in Chapter 6) and select Straight (or another interpolation style) and Display Markers.

To change the style of markers in a chart, select a marker series in the chart and from the menus choose:

Attributes
  Marker

This opens the Markers palette, as shown in Figure 8.6.

Figure 8.6   Marker palette

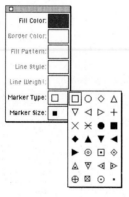

Drag the pointer to the marker type you want and release it. When you release the mouse button, the selected series changes to the new marker type.

The speed of drawing scatterplots on the screen may vary with the type of marker. Squares and triangles tend to be faster than circles on a computer with a graphics accelerator. Hollow markers tend to be faster than filled ones.

Apply All. You can change the marker type for only the selected series or for all of the series at once. To apply a selection to all series in the chart, hold down the command key ⌘ while selecting the marker type.

Marker Size

To change the size of markers in a chart, select a series of markers and from the menus choose:

Attributes
  Marker Size

This opens the Marker Size palette, as shown in Figure 8.7.

Figure 8.7   Marker Size palette

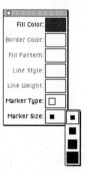

Drag the pointer to the size you want and release it. By default, each series appears in the small size.

Apply All. You can change the marker size for only the selected series or for all of the series at once. To apply a marker size to all series in the chart, hold down the command key ⌘ while selecting the marker size.

Changing Text Objects

You can change the font, font attributes (bold, italic, etc.), or point size of a text object. Text objects include titles, footnotes, axis titles, axis labels for a single axis, legend text, and annotations. Selection is indicated by a selection rectangle surrounding the text.

Font. To change the font of a text object in a chart, first select the text object. Then, from the Font menu, select a font. The selected font is indicated by a check mark.

Size. To change the size of a text object in a chart, first select the text object. Then, from the Size menu, select or enter a size.

9 Printing

This chapter describes how to print files. You can print:

- Text files from syntax or output windows.
- Data files from the Data Editor window.
- Chart files from chart windows and the Chart Carousel.

Printing Output and Syntax

You can print a whole syntax or output file or a selected portion. To print an output or syntax text file:

1. Make the window containing the file the active window.

2. From the menus choose:

   File
     Print...

   This opens a standard dialog box for printing files. The dialog box displayed depends on the selected printer. Figure 9.1 shows the LaserWriter print dialog box.

   Figure 9.1   Print dialog box

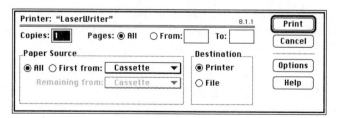

3. To print the file, click on Print.

Printing a Range of Pages

You can print a range of pages. However, output page numbers displayed in SPSS will not correspond to the From and To page numbers in the print dialog box if:

- Any output pages have been deleted between the beginning of the output file and the specified page range.
- Any output extends beyond the displayed right page border in the output window.

Printing a Selection

To print a highlighted selection of output or syntax:

1. Highlight the selection you want to print.

2. From the menus choose:

   File
     Print Selection

The selection is printed without opening a print dialog box.

Printing a Data File

To print a data file, follow the same steps used to print a syntax or output file. You can print the entire file, a range of pages, or a selected area.

Options for Data Files

You can print or suppress grid lines that outline data cells. You can also print actual data values or value labels that have been defined.

A data file is printed as it appears on screen. Whether grid lines and value labels are printed depends on whether they appear in the Data Editor window.

Grid Lines

By default, grid lines are displayed. To turn grid lines off and on:

1. Make the Data Editor window the active window.

2. From the menus choose:

   Utilities
     Grid Lines

Value Labels

By default, value labels are not displayed. To turn value labels on and off:

1. Make the Data Editor window the active window.

2. From the menus choose:

   Utilities
     Value Labels

When value labels are turned on, all values for which a label is defined appear as the label. A label wider than the cell in which it appears is truncated.

Format of Printed Data Files

Printed data files are paginated from left to right and top to bottom. Page numbers in the form *row–column* are displayed. For example, page 1–1 contains the top rows of data in the first set of columns from the left. Page 2–2 contains data in the second set of rows from the top in the second set of columns from the left. Variable names and case numbers are printed on every page.

Printing a Chart File

To print a chart file:

1. Make the chart window or the Chart Carousel the active window.

2. From the menus choose:

   File
     Print...

This opens a standard dialog box for printing files. The dialog box displayed depends on the selected printer.

The following options are available for printing charts:

❑ **Redraw image for printer**. Redraws chart to adjust for printer fonts. If your chart uses fonts or font sizes that are not loaded in the printer, the printer uses the closest available font and size, and text may be truncated or may not be aligned properly with the chart unless the chart is first redrawn for the printer. This option produces the best printed results, but it can be slow. Deselect this default option if you want only a quick draft or if your chart uses only printer fonts.

Redrawing a chart for printing also allows you to adjust the following chart features:

Aspect Ratio. The width-to-height ratio of the outer frame of the chart. You can choose one of the following alternatives:

❍ **As is**. Uses the chart aspect ratio as it appears in the chart on the screen. (Chart aspect ratio is controlled from the Preferences Graphics dialog box. See Chapter 11.)

❍ **Best for printer**. Makes full use of an 8 1/2 × 11-inch page in landscape (horizontal) mode.

Printing a Range of Pages

You can use the From and To page range specifications in the print dialog box to print a selected range of charts in the Chart Carousel. The From and To page numbers correspond to the order of the charts in the Chart Carousel.

Production Mode Printing

Automatic printing of output and charts is available in production mode. For more information, see Appendix A.

10 Utilities

This chapter describes the functions found on the Utilities menu.

Command Index

If you are familiar with SPSS command syntax, you can quickly find the corresponding dialog boxes using the Command Index. From the menus choose:

Utilities
  Command Index...

This opens the Command Index dialog box, as shown in Figure 10.1.

Figure 10.1 Command Index dialog box

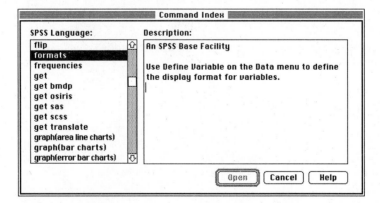

SPSS Language. Displays a complete list of SPSS commands in alphabetical order. To go to the corresponding dialog box for a command, select the command from the list and click on Open (or double-click on the command name).

Description. Provides a brief description of the command and its availability. Some commands are not part of the Base system and require add-on options; others cannot be accessed through dialog boxes. The description identifies optional features and commands that can be run only by entering syntax in a syntax window.

Fonts

To change the type font used in a syntax or output window or in the Data Editor window, make the window the active window, and from the menus choose:

Utilities
  Fonts...

This opens the Font dialog box, as shown in Figure 10.2.

Figure 10.2   Font dialog box

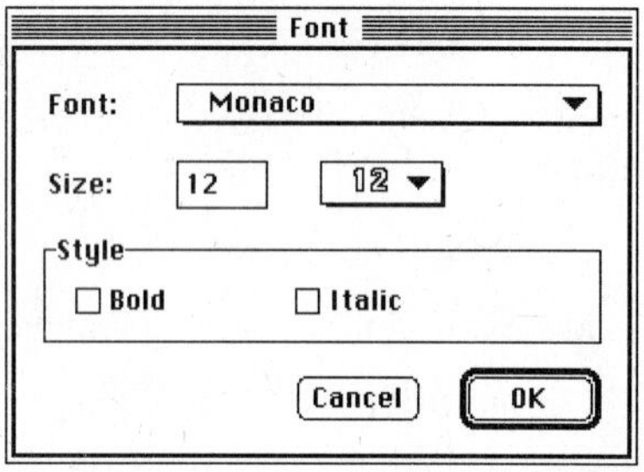

Font. Lists all of the available fixed-pitch fonts for syntax and output windows. Lists all available fonts for the Data Editor.

Size. Lists available point sizes for the selected font.

Style. You can select Bold or Italic or both.

Font changes are applied to all text in the active window. Fonts cannot be selectively applied to portions of a file.

Variable Information

To obtain information on individual variables, copy and paste variable names into command syntax, or go to a specific variable in the Data Editor window, from the menus choose:

Utilities
  Variables...

This opens the Variables dialog box, as shown in Figure 10.3.

Figure 10.3   Variables dialog box

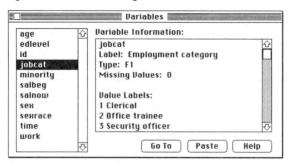

The Variable Information box displays variable definition information for the currently selected variable, including:

- Data format
- Variable label
- User-missing values
- Value labels

You can modify the definition of a variable using the Define Variable dialog box (see Chapter 3).

In addition to variable information, the following options are available:

Go To. To find the selected variable in the Data Editor window, click on Go To. This closes the Variables dialog box and makes the Data Editor the active window.

Paste. To paste variable names into command syntax:

1. If you have more than one syntax window open, make the syntax window into which you want to paste the variable names the designated syntax window.

2. Position the cursor where you want the variable names to be pasted.

3. Highlight the variables in the Variables dialog box and click on Paste. You can also paste individual variables simply by double-clicking on them.

Variable Sets

You can restrict the variables that appear on dialog box source variable lists by defining and using variable sets.

Defining Variable Sets

To define variable sets, from the menus choose:

Utilities
  Define Sets...

This opens the Define Variable Sets dialog box, as shown in Figure 10.4.

Figure 10.4   Define Variable Sets dialog box

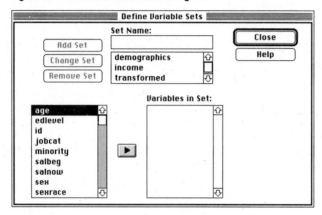

You can create new sets, modify existing sets, and remove sets.

- To create a new set, enter a set name, select the variables to include in the set, and click on Add Set.
- To modify an existing set or change the set name, select the set name from the list of sets, make the changes, and click on Change Set.
- To remove a set, select the set name from the list of sets and click on Remove Set.

Set Name. Set names can be up to 12 characters long. Any characters, including blanks, can be used. Set names are not case sensitive. If you enter the name of an existing set, Add Set is disabled and Change Set is enabled, indicating that the new set definition will replace an existing set.

Variables in Set. Any combination of numeric, short string, and long string variables can be included in a set. The order of variables in the set has no effect on the display order of the variables on dialog box source lists. A variable can belong to multiple sets.

Using Variable Sets

To use variable sets, from the menus choose:

Utilities
  Use Sets...

This opens the Use Sets dialog box, as shown in Figure 10.5.

Figure 10.5   Use Sets dialog box

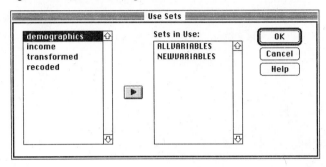

The source list contains any defined variable sets for the data file.

Sets in Use. Displays the sets used to produce the source variable lists in dialog boxes. Variables appear on the source lists in alphabetical or file order. The order of sets and the order of variables within a set have no effect on source list variable order. By default, two system-defined sets are in use:

- **ALLVARIABLES**. This set contains all variables in the data file, including new variables created during a session.

- **NEWVARIABLES**. This set contains only new variables created during the session.

You can remove these sets from the list and select others, but there must be at least one set on the list. If you don't remove the ALLVARIABLES set from the Sets in Use list, any other sets you include are more or less irrelevant.

File Information

To display complete dictionary information for every variable in the currently open data file, from the menus choose:

Utilities
  File Info

The following information is displayed in the output window:

- Variable name.
- Descriptive variable label (if any).
- Print and write formats. The data type is followed by a number indicating the maximum width and the number of decimal positions (if any). For example, F8.2 indicates a numeric variable with a maximum width of eight columns, including one column for the decimal point and two columns for decimal positions.
- Descriptive value labels (if any) for different values of the variable. Both the value and the corresponding label are displayed.

Output Page Titles

SPSS can place a heading at the top of each page in output files. The default heading includes the date, page number, and the version of SPSS being used. To add a title or subtitle to the output page heading, from the menus choose:

Utilities
  Output Page Titles...

This opens the Output Page Title dialog box, as shown in Figure 10.6.

Figure 10.6   Output Page Title dialog box

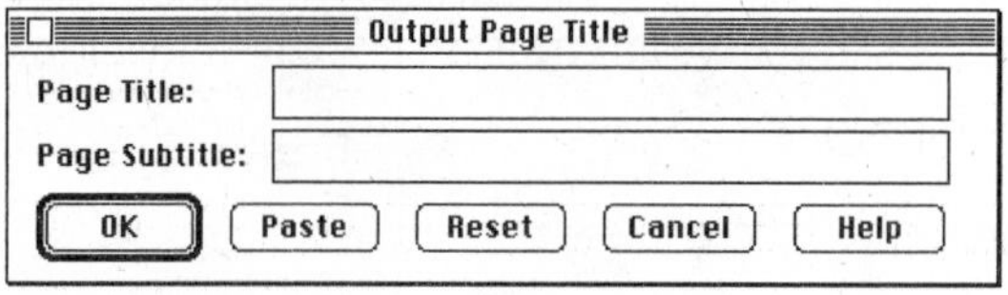

Page Title. The title can be up to 60 characters in length.

Page Subtitle. The subtitle can be up to 60 characters in length.

You can use quotation marks or apostrophes in your title or subtitle, but not both.

New titles and subtitles affect only new output and take effect on the next display page. If you want different titles for different analyses, enter a new title before running each analysis. Titles affect all output windows.

Displaying Output Page Titles

Output page titles and subtitles appear on output pages only if you choose to display full page headers. To turn on the display of full page headers, from the menus choose:

Edit
  Preferences...

This opens the Preferences dialog box. Click on Output to open the Preferences Output dialog box, and click on Full in the Page Headers group to display page titles. For more information on output preferences, see Chapter 11.

Stopping the SPSS Processor

If you inadvertently select a statistical analysis that you don't want, you can stop the SPSS Processor. This is particularly useful if you are working with a large data file or if you have requested statistics for a large number of variables and the procedure takes a long time to execute. To halt the execution of a procedure, from the menus choose:

File
  Stop SPSS Processor

Other Utilities

The Utilities menu also contains the following features:

Grid Lines. Turns the display of grid lines in the Data Editor on and off.

Value Labels. Turns the display of value labels in the Data Editor on and off.

Auto New Case. Automatically creates new cases in the Data Editor.

Designate Window. Makes the active syntax or output window the designated window. Output is routed to the designated output window; command syntax is pasted into the designated syntax window.

11 Preferences

Many of the SPSS default settings can be replaced by user-specified values. Most of these changes remain in effect only for the duration of the session. However, some changes are persistent across SPSS sessions. These persistent default modifications are called **preferences**, and you can customize these preferences to meet your specific needs. These preferences include:

- Content and location of the SPSS journal file
- Special workspace allocation
- Custom currency formats
- Plot symbols used in character-based charts and plots
- Colors, patterns, and other default preferences for high-resolution charts
- Output page width and length
- System information displayed in output windows

To modify the SPSS preference settings during a session, from the menus choose:

Edit
  Preferences...

This opens the Preferences dialog box, as shown in Figure 11.1.

Figure 11.1 Preferences dialog box

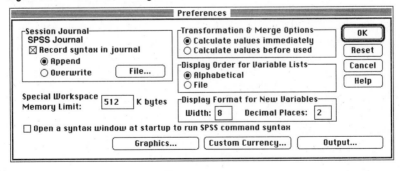

Session Journal

SPSS automatically creates and maintains a journal file of all commands run in an SPSS session. This includes commands entered and run in syntax windows and commands generated by dialog box choices. You can edit the journal file and use the commands again in other SPSS sessions.

❏ **Record syntax in journal.** Any SPSS command syntax generated in the session is recorded in the journal file. This is the default. You can turn the journal off and on during the session, saving selected sets of commands.

○ **Append.** Saves a journal of all SPSS sessions. The command syntax for each successive SPSS session is appended to the bottom of the journal file. This is the default.

○ **Overwrite.** Saves a journal of only the most recent SPSS session. Each time you start a new session, the journal file is overwritten.

Journal Filename and Location

By default, SPSS creates a journal file named SPSS Journal in the SPSS application folder. To change the filename or folder, click on File in the Preferences dialog box. This opens a standard dialog box for selecting files.

Workspace Allocation

Working memory is allocated as needed during the execution of most commands. However, there are a few procedures that take all of the available workspace at the beginning of execution. To optimize performance, SPSS has set some limitations on the size of "all." This limit can be any size you specify, either in the Preferences dialog box as the Special Workspace Memory Limit or on the SET command in a syntax window.

Special Workspace Memory Limit. Maximum virtual memory allocated to workspace. Specify a memory limit in this text box when you get a message stating that you should change the workspace allocation. The new workspace allocation takes effect as soon as you click on OK. After you are finished with the procedure, you should probably reduce the limit to its previous amount. The default value is 512K.

The following procedures are affected by the special workspace memory limit:

- Frequencies
- Crosstabs
- Means
- Nonparametric Tests (Chi-Square, Binomial Test, Runs Test, etc.)

Each of these procedures may display a message in the output stating what can be done within the memory limits specified. If you get a message stating that you should change the workspace allocation, you can change the limit in the Preferences dialog box. To decide on a new value, use the information that is displayed in the output window before the out-of-memory message.

You can also use the WORKSPACE subcommand on the SET command (see the *SPSS Base System Syntax Reference Guide*) to set the workspace limit.

Memory Allocation

If you cannot allocate enough memory with the special workspace memory or you need to allocate more memory for procedures not covered by the special workspace memory, you can also increase the preferred memory size for the SPSS Processor.

1. Click on the SPSS Processor icon in the Finder. This should be located in the SPSS folder, inside the Preferences folder of the System folder, as shown in Figure 11.2.

2. From the menu bar, choose:

   File
     Get Info

3. Increase the Preferred size in the Memory Requirements of the SPSS Processor Info window, as shown in Figure 11.2.

4. Restart SPSS.

Figure 11.2   Increasing memory allocation for the SPSS Processor

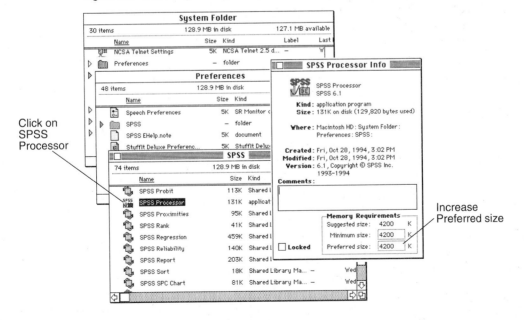

Open a Syntax Window at Startup

Syntax windows are text windows used to enter, edit, and run SPSS commands. If you frequently work with command syntax, select Open a syntax window at startup to automatically open a syntax window at the beginning of each SPSS session. This is useful primarily for experienced SPSS users who prefer to work with command syntax instead of dialog boxes.

Transformation and Merge Options

Each time SPSS executes a command, it reads the data file. Some data transformations (for example, Compute and Recode) and file transformations (Add Variables and Add Cases) do not require a separate pass of the data, and execution of these commands can be delayed until SPSS reads the data to execute another command, such as a statistical procedure. There are two alternatives for the treatment of these transformations:

○ **Calculate values immediately**. Executes the requested transformation and reads the data file. This is the default. If the data file is large and you have multiple transformations, this may be time consuming.

○ **Calculate values before used**. Delays execution of all transformations until SPSS encounters a command that requires a data pass. If the data file is large, this can save a significant amount of processing time. However, pending transformations limit what you can do in the Data Editor (see the *SPSS Base System User's Guide, Part 2*).

Display Order for Variable Lists

There are two alternatives for the display order of variables on dialog box source variable lists:

○ **Alphabetical**. Displays variables in alphabetical order. This is the default.

○ **File**. Displays variables in file order. This is the same order in which variables are displayed in the Data Editor window.

A change in variable display order takes effect the next time you open a data file. Display order affects only source variable lists. Selected variable lists always reflect the order in which variables were selected.

Display Format for New Variables

The default display format for new variables applies only to numeric variables. There is no default display format for new string variables.

Width. Total display width (including decimal positions) for new numeric variables. The maximum total width is 40 characters. The default is 8.

Decimal Places. Number of decimal positions for new numeric variables. The maximum number of decimal positions is 16. The default is 2.

If a value is too large for the specified display format, SPSS first rounds decimal places and then converts values to scientific notation. Display formats do not affect internal data values. For example, the value 123456.78 may be rounded to 123457 for display, but the original unrounded value is used in any calculations.

Graphics

To specify new default setting for high-resolution graphics (charts and plots that appear in the Chart Carousel and chart windows), click on Graphics in the Preferences dialog box. This opens the Preferences Graphics dialog box, as shown in Figure 11.3.

Figure 11.3   Preferences Graphics dialog box

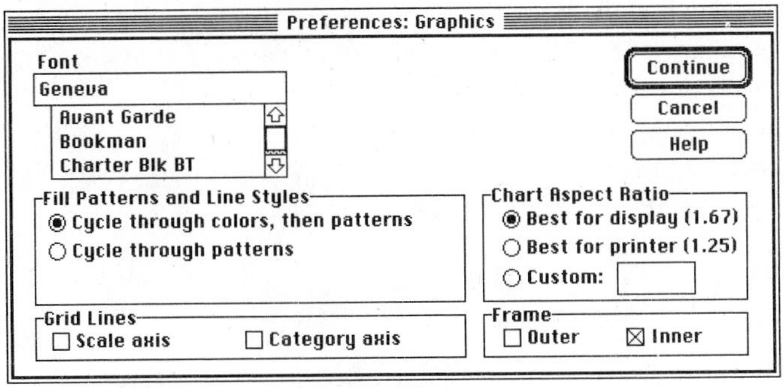

With the exception of changes in Chart Aspect Ratio, any changes that you make in the default settings affect only new charts and charts still in the Chart Carousel. Charts in chart windows are not affected.

Note: Some chart modifications may cause some chart attributes to revert to the Preferences default settings. These modifications include changing chart types (Gallery menu) and transposing data (Series menu).

Font. The initial type font for new charts. Select a font from the list.

Fill Patterns and Line Styles. The initial assignment of colors and/or patterns for new charts. You can choose one of the following alternatives:

○ **Cycle through colors, then patterns**. Use the default palette of 14 colors and then add patterns to colors.

○ **Cycle through patterns**. Use patterns only. Do not use colors. For line charts, the cycle includes 4 line styles within 4 line weights to make 16 possible combinations. For bar charts, area charts, and pie charts, the cycle includes 39 fill patterns. For scatterplots, the cycle includes 28 available marker types.

Grid Lines. You can choose one or both of the following:

❑ **Scale axis**. Displays horizontal grid lines on the scale axis.

❑ **Category axis**. Displays vertical grid lines on the category axis.

Chart Aspect Ratio. The width-to-height ratio of the outer frame of charts. Charts displayed in chart windows, as well as new charts and charts in the Chart Carousel, are affected by a change in the Chart Aspect Ratio box. You can choose one of the following for the width-to-height ratio of charts:

○ **Best for display (1.67)**. The aspect ratio for a full-size chart window on a 640 × 480 (VGA) resolution monitor.

○ **Best for printer (1.25)**. This makes full use of an 8 1/2 × 11-inch page in landscape (horizontal) mode.

○ **Custom**. You can specify your own width-to-height ratio from 0.5 to 2.0. Values below 1 make charts that are taller than they are wide. Values over 1 make charts that are wider than they are tall. A value of 1 produces a square chart.

Frame. You can choose one or both of the following:

❑ **Outer**. Draws a frame around the entire chart, including titles and legends.

❑ **Inner**. Draws a frame around the graphic portion of the chart.

Custom Currency Formats

You can specify up to five custom currency display formats. To create a custom currency format, click on Custom Currency in the Preferences dialog box. This opens the Preferences Custom Currency Formats dialog box, as shown in Figure 11.4.

Figure 11.4   Preferences Custom Currency Formats dialog box

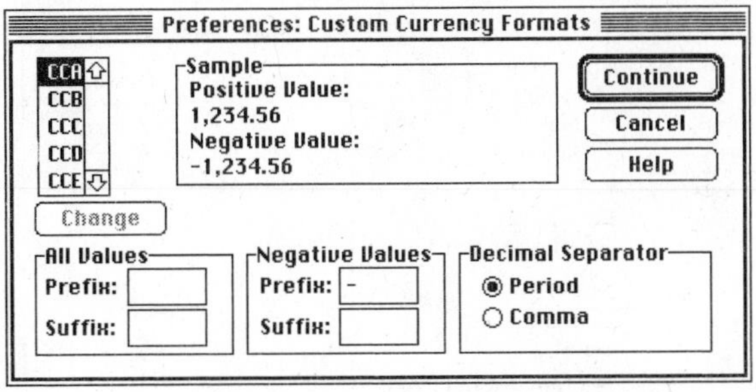

The five custom currency format names are CCA, CCB, CCC, CCD, and CCE. You cannot change the format names or add new ones. By default, all five custom currency formats use a minus sign for the negative prefix and do not have a negative suffix. To modify a custom currency format, select the format name from the source list, make the desired changes, and then click on Change.

All Values. Prefix and suffix specifications appear with both positive and negative values.

Negative Values. Prefix and suffix specifications appear only with negative values. For example, you may want to indicate negative values with parentheses instead of a leading minus sign.

Decimal Separator. The decimal indicator can be either a period or a comma.

Output

Output preferences affect the text-based results of your SPSS session displayed in the output windows. Changes to output preferences affect all output windows. Changes to output preferences affect only output generated after the modification is made; output generated earlier in the session is not affected.

To modify the display of system information, page-size specifications, symbols used in character-based plots, and borders for tabular data, click on Output in the Preferences dialog box. This opens the Preferences Output dialog box, as shown in Figure 11.5.

Figure 11.5   Preferences Output dialog box

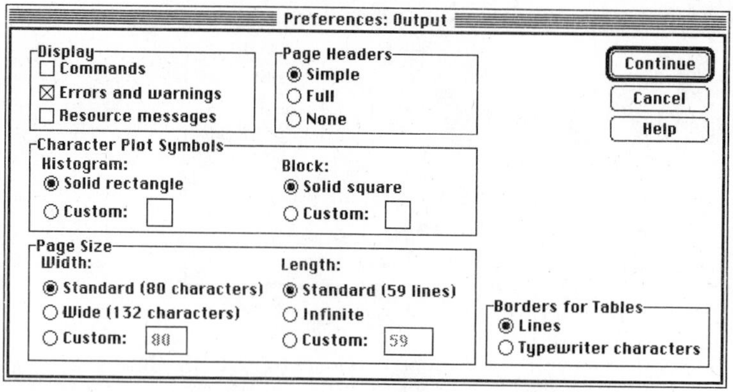

```
╔══════════════════════════════════════════════════════════╗
║                   Preferences: Output                      ║
╟──────────────────────────────────────────────────────────╢
║  ┌─Display─────────────┐  ┌─Page Headers─┐                 ║
║  │ ☐ Commands          │  │ ◉ Simple     │   ┌──────────┐  ║
║  │ ☒ Errors and warnings│ │ ○ Full       │   │ Continue │  ║
║  │ ☐ Resource messages │  │ ○ None       │   └──────────┘  ║
║  └─────────────────────┘  └──────────────┘   ┌──────────┐  ║
║  ┌─Character Plot Symbols─────────────────┐  │  Cancel  │  ║
║  │ Histogram:          Block:             │  └──────────┘  ║
║  │ ◉ Solid rectangle   ◉ Solid square     │  ┌──────────┐  ║
║  │                                        │  │   Help   │  ║
║  │ ○ Custom: [    ]    ○ Custom: [    ]   │  └──────────┘  ║
║  └────────────────────────────────────────┘                ║
║  ┌─Page Size──────────────────────────────┐                ║
║  │ Width:              Length:            │                ║
║  │ ◉ Standard (80 characters) ◉ Standard (59 lines)         ║
║  │ ○ Wide (132 characters)  ○ Infinite    │ ┌Borders for Tables┐
║  │ ○ Custom: [80]   ○ Custom: [59]        │ │ ◉ Lines          │
║  │                                        │ │ ○ Typewriter characters│
║  └────────────────────────────────────────┘                ║
╚══════════════════════════════════════════════════════════╝
```

Display. In addition to the results of statistical procedures, SPSS can also display a variety of system information in the output windows.

❑ **Commands**. Displays SPSS command syntax in the output window. Most dialog box choices generate underlying SPSS command syntax, and it is often helpful to have a record of how certain results were obtained.

❑ **Errors and warnings**. Displays all SPSS error and warning messages in the output window. These are displayed by default. Deselect this item to suppress the display of error and warning messages.

❑ **Resource messages**. Displays resource utilization messages, including elapsed time, available memory, and memory required to run each statistical procedure.

Page Headers. This controls the display of page markers, titles, and subtitles in output windows.

○ **Simple**. Inserts page markers between output pages and starts output from each procedure on a new page. Output page titles are not displayed. This is the default.

○ **Full**. Inserts page markers between output pages, starts output from each procedure on a new page, and displays output page titles and subtitles.

○ **None**. Turns off page headers. Page markers are not inserted between output pages, new output blocks can start anywhere on a page, and output page titles and subtitles are not displayed.

Character Plot Symbols. For low-resolution, character-based charts and plots, you can select the plot symbols used in the output display.

Histogram. You can choose one of the following alternatives for histogram plot characters:

○ **Solid rectangle**. Uses graphical characters to display a solid rectangle. This is the default.

○ **Custom**. User-specified, standard typewriter character. Only one character can be specified. For example, each bar of the histogram can be represented by a string of asterisks.

Block. You can choose one of the following alternatives for block characters used in bar charts and icicle plots:

○ **Solid square**. Uses graphical characters to display solid squares for bar charts and icicle plots. This is the default.

○ **Custom**. User-specified standard typewriter character. Only one character can be specified. For example, each bar can be represented by a string of pound signs (#).

Use the Custom options for plotting symbols to specify standard typewriter characters if you want to open the output file later in another software application.

Page Size. In SPSS, page size is defined by the number of characters per line and the number of lines per page. The default settings of 80 characters per line and 59 lines per page are based on the default font size (10 pt.) and the default paper size and orientation (8 1/2 × 11, portrait). For more information on fonts and printing, see Chapter 9.

Width. You can choose one of the following alternatives for width:

○ **Standard**. 80 characters per line. This is the default.

○ **Wide**. 132 characters per line.

○ **Custom**. User-specified number of characters per line. The minimum is 80. The maximum is 255.

Length. You can choose one of the following alternatives for length:

○ **Standard**. 59 lines per page. This is the default.

○ **Infinite**. Output appears as one continuous page.

○ **Custom**. User-specified number of lines per page. The minimum is 24. The maximum is 9999.

Borders for Tables. You can use either extended ASCII characters or standard typewriter characters to create borders around crosstabulations and other tabular output.

○ **Lines.** Uses graphical characters to create solid horizontal and vertical lines for tables. This is the default.

○ **Typewriter characters.** Uses standard typewriter characters to create horizontal and vertical borders for tables. The dash (–) is used for horizontal lines, the vertical bar symbol (|) is used for vertical lines, and the plus sign (+) is used for the intersection of vertical and horizontal lines. Select this option if you want to open the output file later in another software application.

Using SPSS Graphical Characters

SPSS uses a special graphical character set not available with other software applications. If you copy output that contains graphical characters from SPSS into another application via the clipboard, SPSS automatically converts these graphical characters to standard typewriter characters.

• Table borders are converted to a dash (–) for horizontal lines, a vertical bar symbol (|) for vertical lines, and a plus sign (+) for the intersection of vertical and horizontal lines.

• The solid rectangle used in character-based histograms is converted to an asterisk (*).

• The solid square used in character-based bar charts and icicle plots is converted to a capital letter X.

12 Getting Help

SPSS uses a hypertext Help system to provide information you need to use SPSS and to understand the results. This chapter contains a brief description of the Help system and the kinds of help provided with SPSS.

The best way to find out more about the Help system is to use it. You can ask for help in any of these ways:

- Click on the Help pushbutton in an SPSS dialog box.
- Select SPSS Help from the Help menu.
- Use Balloon Help for information about the toolbar, SPSS menus, and dialog boxes that don't have a Help pushbutton.
- Use the toolbar for help on SPSS terms (glossary tool) and command syntax (syntax tool).

Inside SPSS Help

When a Help window (see Figure 12.1) is active, you can move from topic to topic with the pushbuttons across the top of the window: Topics, Previous, Keyword, << (browse backward), >> (browse forward), and Search.

Figure 12.1   Help window

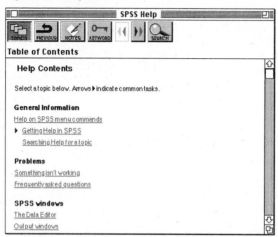

Within the text of a Help topic, there are hypertext links to other topics. These appear as underlined words and may be in color. Some of them cause SPSS Help to display another topic (you can return with the Previous button). Others cause another topic to "pop up" in front of the current one until you click the mouse or press a key.

Searching for a Help Topic

You can search for topics in the Help system in two ways:

- Keyword search provides an index of keywords and related topics for each keyword. Click on a keyword to display the list of related topics, and then click on a topic to go directly to that topic.

- Full-text search finds every occurrence of a text string and displays a list of topics that contain the text string. Since the SPSS Help system is quite extensive, full-text search can take a considerable amount of time.

Copying Help Text

You can copy any Help topic to the clipboard. To copy Help text, from the Help menu bar choose:

Edit
  Select All

and then

Edit
  Copy

You can then paste the text into an output window, a syntax window, a text editor, or a word processor.

Types of Help Available

The SPSS Help system provides the following types of assistance:

Help for dialog boxes. Most SPSS dialog boxes have a Help pushbutton that takes you directly to a topic describing the use of that dialog box. This is the fastest way to learn how to use a dialog box.

 Help menu. The SPSS Help selection on the Help menu takes you to the table of contents of the Help system.

Balloon Help. Turn on Balloon Help for information on the toolbar, SPSS menus, and dialog boxes that don't have a Help pushbutton.

 Output glossary. The SPSS glossary contains definitions of terms that appear in the statistical output displayed by SPSS. Highlight the term in the output window, and then click on the glossary tool on the SPSS toolbar.

SPSS Command Syntax Charts

 Syntax diagrams for the SPSS command language are available to assist you if you work with command syntax in a syntax window. Click on the syntax tool on the toolbar, and then select a command from the scrolling list. If the window already contains command syntax, the syntax tool takes you directly to the diagram for the command you are working on. Figure 12.2 shows a syntax Help window.

Figure 12.2   Syntax Help window

```
▤□                          SPSS Help                          ▤▥
┌──────┬──────┬──────┬──────┬─────┬─────┬──────┐
│ TOPICS│PREVIOUS│NOTES│KEYWORD│ ◀◀ │ ▶▶ │SEARCH│
└──────┴──────┴──────┴──────┴─────┴─────┴──────┘
Regression command syntax
┌──────────────────────────────────────────────────────┬─┐
│ Regression Syntax                                      │⬆│
│                                                        │ │
│ REGRESSION [MATRIX=[IN({file})] [OUT({file})]]         │ │
│             {* }     {* }                              │ │
│ [/VARIABLES={varlist }]                                │ │
│        {(COLLECT)**}                                   │ │
│        {ALL       }                                    │ │
│ [/DESCRIPTIVES=[DEFAULTS][MEAN][STDDEV][CORR][COV]     │ │
│        [VARIANCE][XPROD][SIG][N][BADCORR]              │ │
│        [ALL][NONE**]]                                  │ │
│ [/SELECT={varname relation value}                      │ │
│ [/MISSING=[{LISTWISE**   }] [INCLUDE]]                 │ │
│        {PAIRWISE }                                     │ │
│        {MEANSUBSTITUTION}                              │ │
│ [/WIDTH={132**}]                                       │ │
│        {n  }                                           │ │
│ [/REGWGT=varname]                                      │ │
│ [/STATISTICS=[DEFAULTS**][R**][COEFF**]                │ │
│        [ANOVA**][OUTS**]                               │ │
│        [ZPP][CHA][CI][F][BCOV]                         │⬇│
│        [SES][LINE][HISTORY][XTX][COLLIN]               │▣│
└──────────────────────────────────────────────────────┴─┘
```

Appendix A
Production Mode

When you start an SPSS session by double-clicking on the SPSS application icon in the SPSS folder on the desktop, you interactively analyze data using menus or SPSS command syntax. Based on examination of results, you can perform additional analyses in the same session.

In **Production Mode**, you submit a syntax file containing command syntax to the SPSS Production Mode application, represented by a separate icon in the SPSS folder, and it automatically produces an output file and any charts requested. This mode is useful if you often run the same set of time-consuming analyses, such as weekly reports. Using SPSS Production Mode requires some knowledge of SPSS command syntax (see the *SPSS Base System Syntax Reference Guide*).

While running SPSS Production Mode, you cannot run SPSS at the same time. However, you can run other applications.

Running SPSS in Production Mode

You can run a command syntax file (job file) in Production Mode by dropping a command syntax file on the SPSS Production Mode icon, by running the SPSS Production Mode application, or by using AppleScript:

Drag and drop. Drag the job file icon and drop it on the Production Mode icon in the SPSS folder. After the job has been run, the Production Mode application quits.

Run the Production Mode application. You can run the job file by following these steps:

1. Double-click the Production Mode icon to start the application.

2. From the menus choose:

   File
     Run Syntax...

3. From the standard file selection dialog box, select the command syntax file you want to run.

After the job is done by using this method, the Production Mode application remains open, ready to run another command syntax file.

Use AppleScript. AppleScript is an operating system extension. It is part of System 7.1 Pro or System 7.5. It is also available as a commercial application. To run an SPSS command syntax file, you can supply a filename and run the following command in the AppleScript Script Editor:

`tell application "SPSS Production Mode" to RunSyntax "filename"`

For example:

`tell application "SPSS Production Mode" to RunSyntax "Macintosh HD:SPSS 6.1:Daily Jobs:Survey Job"`

If SPSS Production Mode is not already running, this command starts SPSS Production Mode, runs the specified job, and quits Production Mode. If SPSS Production Mode is already running, the command simply runs the syntax file, queuing as necessary.

SPSS Production Mode supports three scripting events:

Run	*Starts SPSS Production Mode.*
Quit	*Quits SPSS Production Mode.*
RunSyntax _alias_	*Specifies the name of a file to run.* If SPSS Production Mode is not running when it receives a RunSyntax command, it is started, runs the job, and quits. If SPSS Production Mode is already running when it receives the command, it runs the job (queuing if necessary), and continues running after the job ends.

You can use these events to create a custom script that fits your particular circumstances.

Status

While SPSS Production Mode is running, a dialog box displays the status of the job. The information is the same as the command and case counter information that would appear in the status bar of SPSS.

Stopping a Job

To stop a job in progress, click on Stop in the SPSS Production Mode status dialog box. When the job is terminated, SPSS Production Mode remains open.

Output File

SPSS Production Mode creates an output file with the same name as the command syntax file plus the word *output*. For example, for the command syntax file *Production Job*, the output file is *Production Job output*. (Up to 22 characters of the filename are used.) The output contains text results from procedures, errors, warnings, and diagnostics.

The output file is saved by default in the same folder as the command syntax file. If an output file with that name already exists, SPSS Production Mode overwrites the file. Use Production Mode Preferences to change the folder where the output files and chart files are saved.

Chart Files

Each chart is placed in a separate file. Chart names are assigned by adding a sequential number to the command syntax filename. For example, if the root name in Production Mode Preferences is *Production Chart*, SPSS would assign the chart filenames *Production Chart 1*, *Production Chart 2*, *Production Chart 3*, etc. (See "Production Mode Preferences," below.)

The name of an existing chart file with a filename the same as a chart created during the SPSS run is changed by adding *backup* to prevent accidental overwriting. However, an old backup file can be overwritten by the new backup file.

Data Files

If the job contains SAVE, WRITE, or EXPORT commands, these commands determine where to write the data file. If no commands that save data are used, changes in the data file resulting from SPSS transformations or procedures in the job are not saved.

Changing Preferences

SPSS Production Mode defaults are initially set by the preferences in SPSS. For example, you may want to set the font for charts in the Preferences Graphics dialog box in SPSS. In addition, within SPSS Production Mode, you can change certain other preferences.

Production Mode Preferences

To change default settings for SPSS Production Mode, from the menus choose

File
  Preferences...

This opens the Production Mode Preferences dialog box, as shown in Figure A.1.

Figure A.1   Production Mode Preferences dialog box

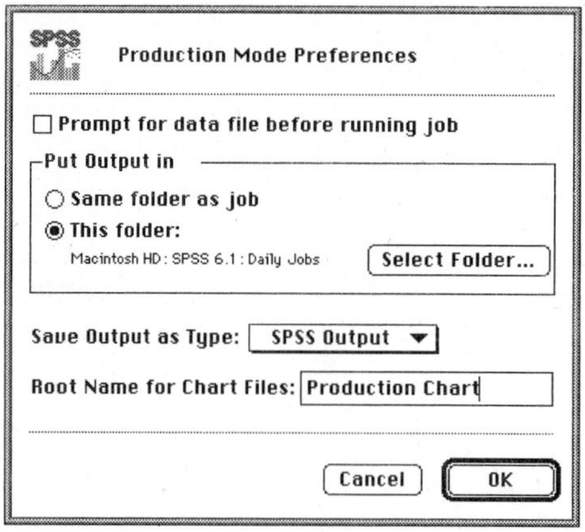

❑ **Prompt for data file before running job.** When this option is selected, each time you run a job, a standard file selection dialog box appears. This option is useful when you save a command syntax file that is independent of the data file used and you want to choose the data file when you are ready to run the job.

Put Output in. By default, the output file and any chart files are saved in the same directory as the command syntax file. You can specify the directory for output and chart files by selecting one of the following choices:

○ **Same folder as job.** This is the default.

○ **This folder.** You can select any folder by clicking on Select Folder and choosing from the standard file selection dialog box.

↴ **Save Output as Type.** You can specify either of two types for the SPSS Output file:

SPSS Output. An SPSS output file uses special line-drawing characters for the lines in items such as tables from the Crosstabs procedure. This is the default. Use this type of file if you expect to use only SPSS to examine or modify the file.

Text. This type of file contains "typewriter" characters to draw the lines in tables. It can be read by any application that can read TEXT files.

Root Name for Chart Files. You can enter up to 27 characters as a root name for charts. For each chart created while running the job, SPSS Production Mode appends a unique sequential number to the root name.

Overriding the Default Working Memory Allocation

The working memory allocation defined in the SPSS Preferences file is used in SPSS Production Mode. For information on how to change the allocation, see Chapter 11.

The default 512K allocation is enough workspace for running most procedures on a moderate-sized data file. In some circumstances, SPSS requires more workspace. For example, you may want a large number of transformations or crosstabulations. SPSS sometimes displays messages to indicate that you must allocate more memory to run a particular job. If you are doing a large number of transformations and you get a message that the job cannot be completed because of insufficient memory, you can estimate how much space is needed. For example, if about half the transformations were done before the message appeared, you can double the amount of workspace. Some messages tell you how much more workspace is needed.

Printing Results

You can print the output file or a chart file in SPSS itself or by using AppleScript.

Printing from SPSS. To print from SPSS, open the output file or chart file in SPSS (not Production Mode). Then select Print from the File menu.

Printing from AppleScript. An alternative method of printing is to use AppleScript with commands such as the following:

```
tell application "SPSS"
repeat with n in (list folder "Macintosh HD:Nightly Output")
  print file ("Macintosh HD:Nightly Output:" & n)
end repeat
end tell
```

The Sample Documents folder installed with SPSS contains a sample AppleScript that combines Production Mode and printing in a single automated process.

Syntax Files

A syntax file containing SPSS command syntax is required for SPSS Production Mode. The syntax must follow the rules for running commands in batch mode:

- Each command must begin in the first column of a new line.
- Continuation lines must be indented at least one space.
- Lines are limited to 80 characters (excluding in-line data).
- The period at the end of the command is optional.

- The job should not contain a FINISH command. A FINISH command will result in a syntax error.

See the *SPSS Base System Syntax Reference Guide* for more information on constructing and running SPSS commands.

If Prompt for data before running job is deselected in Production Mode Preferences, the job must have a command such as GET or IMPORT, or another command that will create a working data file. You can use the SET command and the GRAPH /TEMPLATE command to control the appearance of the output and charts.

Building a Syntax File

One way to build a syntax file is to enter syntax manually and save the syntax file. You can do this in a syntax window in an SPSS session or use any text editor or word processing software that saves files in text format.

There are three ways in which SPSS can help build your syntax file. These methods are usually faster than manually entering command syntax, and they minimize the chance of syntax errors. Each method involves running an SPSS session and saving and editing the command syntax generated in the session.

Pasting Syntax from Dialog Boxes

The easiest way to build command syntax is to paste dialog box selections into a syntax window in a regular SPSS session. To do so, make dialog box choices for the analyses you want to perform. When you click on Paste, command syntax based on your dialog box choices is pasted into a syntax window (for more information on pasting command syntax, see Chapter 4). Save the text file from the syntax window and specify it as the syntax file in Production Mode.

Editing Syntax in an Output File

You can also save command syntax in an output file from an SPSS session that performs the analyses you want. To use this method, in the SPSS Preferences Output dialog box select Commands under Display (see Chapter 11). When SPSS runs your procedure dialog box choices, it writes command syntax to an output file along with the results of your analyses. For example, Figure A.2 shows command syntax and output for descriptive statistics and bivariate correlations procedures.

Figure A.2   Unedited output file

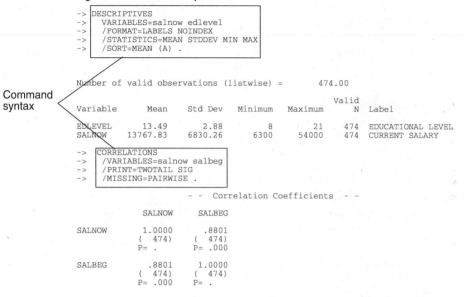

```
->  DESCRIPTIVES
->    VARIABLES=salnow edlevel
->    /FORMAT=LABELS NOINDEX
->    /STATISTICS=MEAN STDDEV MIN MAX
->    /SORT=MEAN (A) .


Number of valid observations (listwise) =        474.00

                                                  Valid
Variable      Mean      Std Dev   Minimum   Maximum     N  Label

EDLEVEL      13.49       2.88         8        21    474  EDUCATIONAL LEVEL
SALNOW    13767.83    6830.26      6300     54000    474  CURRENT SALARY

->  CORRELATIONS
->    /VARIABLES=salnow salbeg
->    /PRINT=TWOTAIL SIG
->    /MISSING=PAIRWISE .

                      - -  Correlation Coefficients  - -

                 SALNOW       SALBEG

SALNOW           1.0000        .8801
               (   474)      (   474)
               P= .          P= .000

SALBEG            .8801       1.0000
               (   474)      (   474)
               P= .000       P= .

(Coefficient / (Cases) / 2-tailed sig)

" . " is printed if a coefficient cannot be computed
```

Command syntax

To create a syntax file, save only the command syntax to a file. You can do this by cutting and pasting the command syntax to another file or deleting everything but the command syntax from the output file. Rectangular selection by using the Option key makes it easy to select the text to be deleted.

Make sure to remove the following:

- Headers
- Titles
- Error and warning messages
- Right arrows (–>) that precede command syntax
- Output markers
- Page break markers

For information on saving without output and page markers, see "Saving Output in Text Format" on p. 71 in Chapter 4. If there are any errors in the output, they must be resolved prior to the Production Mode run or the run will not complete successfully.

Figure A.3 shows an edited version of Figure A.2 that can be used as a syntax file in a Production Mode run. Since Figure A.3 does not contain syntax that opens a data file, in SPSS Production Mode Preferences you must select Prompt for data file before running the job, and then supply a data file name when you run the job.

Figure A.3   Edited output file

```
DESCRIPTIVES
  VARIABLES=salnow edlevel
  /FORMAT=LABELS NOINDEX
  /STATISTICS=MEAN STDDEV MIN MAX
  /SORT=MEAN (A) .

CORRELATIONS
  /VARIABLES=salnow salbeg
  /PRINT=TWOTAIL SIG
  /MISSING=PAIRWISE .
```

Editing Syntax in a Journal File

By default, SPSS records all commands executed during a session in a journal file named *SPSS Journal.* (See Chapter 11 for more information on name, location, and contents of the journal file.)

The journal file is a text file that can be edited like any other text file, and you can create a syntax file by editing the journal file. Remove any error or warning messages. If there are any errors in the output, they must be resolved prior to the Production Mode run or the run will not complete successfully.

Save the edited journal file with a different filename. Since SPSS automatically appends or overwrites the journal file for every session—including Production Mode sessions—attempting to use the same filename for a syntax file and the journal file may yield some unexpected and unwanted results.

Figure A.4 shows a journal file for an SPSS run that opens a data file, creates a variable *y* based on the values of variable *x*, and displays descriptive statistics for each variable. In addition to the SPSS command syntax, there is a data-specific warning message.

Figure A.4   Unedited journal file

```
GET FILE='Hard Disk:SPSS:Programs:MyData' .
EXECUTE .
COMPUTE y = 10 / x .
EXECUTE .
>Warning # 511
>A division by zero has been attempted on the indicated command.  The result
>has been set to the system-missing value.
DESCRIPTIVES
 VARIABLES=x y
 /FORMAT=LABELS NOINDEX
 /STATISTICS=MEAN STDDEV MIN MAX
 /SORT=MEAN (A) .
```

The warning message has been deleted in Figure A.5. Only SPSS command syntax remains in the file.

Figure A.5   Edited journal file

```
GET FILE='Hard Disk:SPSS:Programs:MyData' .
EXECUTE .
COMPUTE y = 10 / x .
EXECUTE .
DESCRIPTIVES
 VARIABLES=x y
 /FORMAT=LABELS NOINDEX
 /STATISTICS=MEAN STDDEV MIN MAX
 /SORT=MEAN (A) .
```

Appendix B
Commands Not Available in SPSS for the Macintosh

Table B.1 and Table B.2 list the SPSS commands and SET subcommands not supported in SPSS for the Macintosh.

Table B.1   Unsupported commands

EDIT	HELP	POINT
FINISH	HOST	SAVE SCSS
GET BMDP	INFO	UNNUMBERED
GET SAS	KEYED DATA LIST	
GET SCSS	NUMBERED	

SPSS for the Macintosh does not support commands that read or save data files in SPSS/PC+ format, as in

GET FILE = 'filename.sys'

SAVE TRANSLATE OUTFILE = 'filename.sys' /TYPE = PC

Table B.2   Unsupported SET subcommands

ENDCMD	SCRIPTTAB	TB2
DUMP	TBFONTS	XSORT
NULLINE	TROFFTAB	
MXERRS	TB1	

Appendix C
Apple Events

Macintosh applications use Apple events to communicate with each other. An Apple event is an instruction that can be sent from one computer application to another. For example, the Finder can use an Apple event to request that another application open or print a document.

You can use Apple events to send instructions to SPSS by using tools such as the AppleScript Script Editor. AppleScript is included with System 7.1 Pro and System 7.5, and is also available as a commercial application. For more information on Apple-Script, see its documentation.

Supported Apple Events

SPSS supports the required suite of Apple events: Open Application, Open Documents, Print Documents, and Quit. These events are described in more detail below. The SPSS system includes a dictionary resource, which you can open in AppleScript.

Run

The Run event (Open Application event) starts SPSS. The script syntax is:

```
run
```

When SPSS receives the Run event, it starts SPSS and opens an untitled data window and an untitled output window. If **Open a syntax window at startup** is selected in SPSS Preferences, a syntax window is also opened. An example of a run command is:

```
run application "SPSS"
```

The Run event can also be communicated in AppleScript by a tell command. For example:

```
tell application "SPSS"
  run
end tell
```

Open Documents

The Open Documents event starts SPSS, if it is not running, and opens one or more SPSS documents. The script syntax is:

open *alias*

If the list contains more than one data document, only the first data document is opened. If there is already a data document open that contains unsaved changes when the Open Document event is received, SPSS asks if you want to save the changes.

TEXT documents not created by SPSS for the Macintosh are opened as syntax documents. An example of a script using the Open Documents event is:

```
tell application "SPSS"
  open file "SPSS data"
end tell
```

Print Documents

The Print Documents event prints one or more SPSS documents. The script syntax is:

print *alias*

If SPSS is *not running* when it receives the Print Documents event, SPSS starts and then prints each document on the list. For each document, SPSS displays the print dialog box for the chosen printer. If you select Cancel in the print dialog box, the printing is canceled and SPSS quits. When all of the documents are printed, SPSS quits.

If SPSS is *already running*, when it receives the Print Documents event, SPSS opens the print dialog box and then prints each document on the list. If the list contains more than one data document, each data document is printed in the order in which it occurs on the list. If there are unsaved changes in a data document, SPSS asks if you want to save the contents of the data window. If you select Cancel in the print dialog box, the printing is canceled and no more documents are printed. An example of the Print Documents event is:

```
tell application "SPSS"
  print file "MacHD:SPSS:SPSS Output"
end tell
```

The Print Documents event can be used to print SPSS output from production mode. (See Appendix A for information about Production Mode.)

Quit Application

The Quit Application event quits SPSS. The script syntax is:

```
quit
```

When SPSS receives the Quit Application event, SPSS asks if you want to save any un-saved changes in the Chart Carousel and each open document window. After the last document is closed, SPSS quits. If you select Cancel in any Save dialog box, the Quit Application process is stopped and SPSS remains open. An example of the Quit Application event is:

```
quit application "SPSS"
```

SPSS Production Mode Events

SPSS Production Mode supports three scripting events:

Run   *Starts SPSS Production Mode.*

Quit   *Quits SPSS Production Mode.*

RunSyntax *alias*   *Specifies the name of a syntax file to run.*

For more information about Production Mode, see Appendix A.

Appendix D
Working with Large Data Files

There is no defined limit to the number of variables that can be contained in an SPSS data file. Using command syntax, the system has been tested with up to 32,000 variables in a data file. However, there is a Macintosh limitation that effectively restricts the number of variables that can be accessed from dialog boxes to approximately 4000 (depending on the length of the variable names). If your file contains a larger number of variables, only the first 4000 will appear on dialog box source lists.

If you need to work with data files that contain more than 4000 variables, you can either enter and run SPSS commands in a syntax window or you can use command syntax to create a subset of variables for use in the dialog box interface.

This appendix provides a brief overview of commands that you can use to read or save a subset of variables from a data file. For information on how to enter and run commands in a syntax window, see Chapter 4. For detailed information on individual commands, see the *SPSS Base System Syntax Reference Guide*.

Using Command Syntax to Create a Subset of Variables

The SPSS commands GET, SAVE, IMPORT, EXPORT, GET TRANSLATE, and MATCH FILES all have two optional subcommands for specifying variables to include or exclude:

- KEEP indicates variables that you want to keep. The order of variables on the KEEP subcommand determines the file order of variables in the working data file.

- DROP indicates variables that you want to drop.

For example, the command

```
GET FILE='big file'
 /KEEP id age income index01 TO index99.
```

creates a working data file with only the specified variables and ignores any other variables that may be contained in the data file *bigfile.sav* (the keyword TO indicates consecutive variables in file order).

If it's easier to specify the variables you *don't* need, use the DROP subcommand, as in:

```
SAVE OUTFILE='notsobig file'
 /DROP shoesize favcolr.
```

Adding Variables and Combining Subsets

There are at least two reasons why you might want or need to add variables from the original data file or combine subsets of variables in the working data file:

- If you create any new variables in the working data file, the only way to use those new variables with other variables not included in the subset is to add the other variables from the original data file or merge the subset with another subset that contains the necessary variables.

- If you split your data file into many, much smaller data files, you can use variables from more than one file by combining the subsets in the working data file.

The MATCH FILES command can handle both of these situations. The following example adds variables from the original data file to the working data file:

```
MATCH FILES FILE=* /FILE='big file'
 /BY id
 /KEEP id TO index99 bigvar1 bigvar3 bigvar5.
```

- The first FILE subcommand indicates the working data file with an asterisk (*).
- The BY subcommand indicates a key variable that is used to match cases.
- The KEEP subcommand lists all variables from both files to keep in the new working data file.
- The keyword TO with the names of the first and last variables in the current working data file includes all of the variables from the current working data file.

If you are combining files that each contain a small subset of variables, and the combined total number of variables in those subsets is less than 4,000, you can use the dialog box interface to combine the files. From the menus choose:

Data
  Merge Files ▶
    Add Variables...

See the *SPSS Base System User's Guide, Part 2* for more information on the Add Variables procedure.

Key Variables and Case Order in Combined Files

The MATCH FILES command assumes that cases appear in the same position in all of the files that are being combined together. If cases are not in the same order or if some cases are present in some files but missing in others, data will be matched incorrectly. To avoid mismatched data, it is strongly recommended that you always use the BY subcommand with one or more **key variables** that uniquely identify each case. The key variables must be present in all of the files being combined, and the files must be sorted in the order of the key variable values.

Index

B = Base System User's Guide, Part 2
R = Base System Syntax Reference Guide